Praise for

Aurora

"Like a master quilter, Jane Kirkpatrick has pieced together scraps of remembrances, letters, and artifacts into an intriguing history of a unique community defined by faith and craft. Quilters especially will enjoy her exploration of the domestic arts and how they enrich the lives of women, past and present."

—JENNIFER CHIAVERINI, author of the Elm Creek Quilts novels

"Jane Kirkpatrick is a remarkable storyteller in her historical novels, but in *Aurora,* she lets the quilts and crafts tell the stories of a Christian communal settlement in nineteenth-century Oregon. She became intimately familiar with these stories in her research for the Change and Cherish Historical Series. This book is a welcome addition, particularly for its photographs and related information on the history of the Aurora Colony."

—JAMES J. KOPP, board member of the Aurora Colony Historical Society and author of *Eden Within Eden: Oregon's Utopian Heritage.*

"*Aurora* brings a warm remembering of one man's effort to establish a caring, sharing community. Jane Kirkpatrick's writing honors the skills and connected lives of a group of people who created a neighborhood, impacting their entire region. Her story inspires readers to hone their skills, simplify their lives, and serve others. The colorful pictures bring a bygone era to life."

—MARY TATEM, author of *Beautiful Threads, The Quilt of Hope,* and the best-selling *The Quilt of Life*

"The Diamond Rule at Oregon's nineteenth-century Aurora Colony was that one should make life better for others. Using her extraordinary gift, Jane Kirkpatrick gives us a story of spirituality and creativity that enriches our lives. Through the agrarian colony's crafts, especially its quilts, Jane re-creates the lives of those pioneers who colonized the western wilderness in a spirit of perseverance, cooperation, and harmony."

—SANDRA DALLAS, author of *Tallgrass* and *The Quilt That Walked to Golden*

"Jane Kirkpatrick brings the Aurora Colony alive through words and pictures. Readers are immersed in the colonists' culture and craft. We can't help but admire how these men and women put beauty into even the most utilitarian objects."

—JUDY BRENEMAN, quilt historian and founder of www.womenfolk.com, celebrating quilts and crafts

"A book on the quilt collection has been a longtime dream of those behind the Aurora Colony Museum. Now with the skills of writer Jane Kirkpatrick, the knowledge of curator Patrick Harris, and the commitment of museum volunteers and members, this book is a reality. Enriched by the expanded focus of family, faith, and community, this project celebrates the same patient energy, perseverance, and cooperation the colonists demonstrated more than one hundred years ago. *Sehr Gut* [very good]!"

—MARY BYWATER CROSS, Oregon quilt historian and author of *Quilts of the Oregon Trail*

"Fascinating and memorable, Jane Kirkpatrick's *Aurora* gives voice to the enduring spirit of our pioneer foremothers and the work of their hands. Anyone interested in our pioneer heritage will love this book. Quilt lovers and historians will want to add it to their libraries."

—STEPHANIE GRACE WHITSON, author of *Unbridled Dreams* and *A Hilltop in Tuscany*, speaker, and quilt historian

"Do you often wonder what lasts after you've gone? *Aurora* shares the legacy left by a creative community who crossed the Oregon Trail to live simply in a new land. These families were drawn together by faith, hard work, and service, as well as by amazing fiber arts, crafts, and culinary delights. Delve into the beautiful pages of this book and savor the quilts that tell a story of not only struggle and sacrifice but also joy and journey. Then do the hard work of examining your own life and tell your own story, leaving a legacy of purpose and grace. *Aurora* is a reminder of what's truly important—that, indeed, 'our lives are the stories others read first.'"

—LUCINDA SECREST MCDOWELL, author of *Quilts from Heaven* and *Role of a Lifetime*

AURORA

Books by Jane Kirkpatrick

NOVELS

A Land of Sheltered Promise

Change and Cherish Historical Series
A Clearing in the Wild
A Tendering in the Storm
A Mending at the Edge

Tender Ties Historical Series
A Name of Her Own
Every Fixed Star
Hold Tight the Thread

Kinship and Courage Historical Series
All Together in One Place
No Eye Can See
What Once We Loved

Dreamcatcher Collection
A Sweetness to the Soul
Love to Water My Soul
A Gathering of Finches
Mystic Sweet Communion

NONFICTION

Homestead: A Memoir of Modern Pioneers Pursuing the Edge of Possibility
A Simple Gift of Comfort (formerly *A Burden Shared*)

ANTHOLOGIES

Daily Guideposts 1992
Storyteller Collection, Book 2
Crazy Woman Creek, "Women Rewrite the American West"

AURORA

An American Experience in Quilt, Community, and Craft

JANE KIRKPATRICK

WATERBROOK
PRESS

AURORA
PUBLISHED BY WATERBROOK PRESS
12265 Oracle Boulevard, Suite 200
Colorado Springs, Colorado 80921

All Scripture quotations, unless otherwise indicated, are taken from the Holy Bible, New International Version®. NIV®. Copyright © 1973, 1978, 1984 by International Bible Society. Used by permission of Zondervan Publishing House. All rights reserved. Scripture quotations marked (ABS) are taken from The Holy Bible, containing the Old and New Testaments, translated out of The Original Tongues, and with the former translations diligently compared and revised. New York: American Bible Society, 1858.

Grateful acknowledgment is made for the use of "Ich bin auf der Welt… / I'm too alone in the world" from *Rilke's Book of Hours: Love Poems to God* by Rainer Maria Rilke, translated by Anita Barrows and Joanna Macy, copyright © 1996 by Anita Barrows and Joanna Macy. Used by permission of Riverhead Books, an imprint of Penguin Group (USA) Inc. Grateful acknowledgment is made for quotations from *Aurora Colony Heritage Recipes*. Used by permission of the Aurora Colony Historical Society. Grateful acknowledgment is made for quotations from *The Complete Book of Everyday Christianity: An A-to-Z Guide to Following Christ in Every Aspect of Life* by Robert Banks and R. Paul Stevens. Used by permission of the authors.

About the cover: This shows detail of a Running Squares quilt with embroidered initials CG, stitched in double crosses by Emma Wagner Giesy in the 1850s. The initials referred to her husband, Christian Giesy, and her son; Emma witnessed her husband's drowning in Willapa Bay, and her descendants say this event marked the remainder of her life, filling it with grief and determination. Worn spots on the quilt show it was used and may have been begun before Emma headed west from Bethel, Missouri, the only woman in that scouting party. After Christian's death and despite her desperate move from Willapa to Aurora in 1861, the quilt remained with her, a treasured artifact.

ISBN 978-1-4000-7428-0

All photos copyright © 2008 by the Aurora Colony Historical Society (ACHS), Janus Childs (JC), Patrick Harris (PH), Jerry Kirkpatrick (JK), or Nancy Lloyd (NL), unless otherwise noted. "Religious Communities" original map copyright © 2008 by Devin Boyle.

Published in the United States by WaterBrook Multnomah, an imprint of The Doubleday Publishing Group, a division of Random House Inc., New York.

WATERBROOK and its deer colophon are registered trademarks of Random House Inc.

Library of Congress Cataloging-in-Publication Data
Kirkpatrick, Jane, 1946–
    Aurora : an American experience in quilt, community, and craft / Jane Kirkpatrick, with the Aurora Colony Historical Society. — 1st ed.
       p. cm.
    Includes bibliographical references and index.
    ISBN 978-1-4000-7428-0
  1. Quilting—Patterns. 2. Patchwork—Patterns. 3. Patchwork quilts—Oregon—Aurora. 4. Aurora Colony (Marion County, Or.)—History. I. Aurora Colony Historical Society. II. Title.
    TT835K524 2008
    746.46'041—dc22

2008023781

Printed in the United States of America
2008—First Edition

10 9 8 7 6 5 4 3 2 1

SPECIAL SALES
Most WaterBrook Multnomah books are available in special quantity discounts when purchased in bulk by corporations, organizations, and special-interest groups. Custom imprinting or excerpting can also be done to fit special needs. For information, please e-mail SpecialMarkets@WaterBrookMultnomah.com or call 1-800-603-7051.

This book is dedicated to the women and men
who express themselves through craft.

The Quilts of Aurora

Appliquéd Birds on Wool

Basket Variation

Bay Leaf / Orange Peel

Bear Paw*

Birds in Flight*

Broken Dishes

Carpenter's Wheel

Cheater Star*

Cookie Cutter

Crazy

Crown of Thorns

Double Irish Chain

Evening Star on Point*

Four Square

Ida's Basket Variation

Indian Hatchet

Grandmother's Fan*

Grandmother's Flower Garden*

Grape Basket*

Log Cabin / Barn Raising

Lost Ships*

Monkey Wrench*

Multichain Variation

Nine Patch

Ocean Waves

Old Maid's Puzzle

Orange Peel

Peaceful Hours

Pine Burr

Pin Wheel*

Running Squares on Point

St. Andrew's Cross*

Streak of Lightning*

Sunflower

Tumbling Blocks

Union Square

Whig's Defeat Variation

* These quilts are not pictured in this book, but they may be available for viewing by appointment in the Aurora Colony Historical Society collection. Quilt names used throughout this book were provided by colonists rather than Barbara Brackman's *Encyclopedia of Pieced Quilt Patterns*.

The Arts and Crafts of Aurora

Animal husbandry

Apple and pear butter production

Baking and cooking

Basket weaving

Blacksmithing

Calling-card design

Canning and food preservation,
including sausage making

Dancing

Distilling

Dyeing and chromatic pigmentation

Furniture making

Home building

Labeling

Leather work

Letter writing

Medicinal herbal healing

Metalworking

Millinery

Musical composition

Musical-instrument making

Musical performance

Photography

Printing

Reed making for musical instruments

Shoemaking

Singing (including folk songs, hymns, chorales)

Spinning wool

Tailoring (including dress, shirt, and suit making)

Textile arts (including Redwork
embroidery, quilt piecing, rug making,
sampler stitching, cross-stitching,
lace making, tatting, and weaving)

Tinsmithing

Toolmaking

Toy making (including miniatures)

Woodcarving

Woodworking

I remember the days of long ago;
I meditate on all your works
and consider what your hands have done.

—Psalm 143:5

To many a soul burning to enjoy the felicities of the blessed has come the inspiration to make earth more endurable by establishing here and now a community that will give to those still on earth a foretaste of the joys in heaven.... The Oneida, Amana, Aurora, and Shaker communities were so conceived and so founded.

—Russell Blankenship, *And There Were Men*

Come and get a goose dinner Sunday as Momma has the goose neck off already. We expect some company, which is by no means unusual at the Giesy ranch. Mama is sewing just now she has all the winter storing in which means a great deal for us or the family.

—a young colonist, Elizabeth Zimmerman,
writing to her aunt

Contents

Craft • *1*

Tumbling Blocks, handquilted by an unknown quilter, was found as stuffing in a couch handed down to the owners of the Keil house. It has 1,365 individual diamond pieces of wool, homespun velvet, and fancier fabric. (ACHS collection.) *JK photo*

Landscapes • *9*

Sunflower was handpieced by Matilda Knight Stauffer. It includes an unbroken plume around the red border and six-point design ("hex wheel") reminiscent of a sand dollar, double-quilted cotton with ten stitches per inch, crosshatching of the center wreath like a sunflower center, and directional quilting toward the border. (Private collection.) *JK photo*

Relationships • *29*

Aurora Keil's handtied Appliquéd Birds on Wool features the bird motif found on hand-crafted colony works; uneven handpieced wool, velveteen, silk, and homespun fabric blocks; and appliquéd bird shapes with a buttonhole stitch. (ACHS collection.) *JK photo*

Work • *71*

This Log Cabin / Barn Raising quilt was handpieced and handquilted by Mary Schuele Rapps, using cotton and wool without batting and a Prairie Points finished edge. For thirty years, Dr. Keil refused permission for Mary to wed Michael Rapps, the butcher, but following Dr. Keil's death, they married. (ACHS collection.) *JK photo*

Faith • *109*

Emma Wagner Giesy handpieced and handquilted Running Squares on Point. With no sashing, it includes block edges run to the border, unique diagonal lines in a sawtooth pattern, and a fan pattern typical of colony quilts. As the only woman scout seeking a new colony site, Emma may have brought the plaids west. (ACHS collection.) *JK Photo*

Prelude

Jane Kirkpatrick has stitched her words into a moving biographical counterpane testifying to the perennial desire of human beings to make useful things beautiful, which I believe is the folk genius of mankind and the wellspring of art.

In recording a segment of Oregon's early territorial history, she has also documented an uncommon experiment to realize humanity's age-old dream of living together in harmony and cooperation. Although conceived in an isolated agrarian format and thereby doomed to a limited and ephemeral success, such a dream, on a grander scale, may yet prove to be the imperative of survival for our planet and its precious cargo of life.

Such values are incongruous in an individualistic society, but we instinctively recognize their importance and are awed by the beauty they have engendered.

I was introduced to Aurora as a young boy when my father, Ivan Houser, sculptor and ceramist, established The Old Colony Town Pottery at its northern approach in the mid-1950s. The building was held together by handforged, square nails, which I could remove with my fingers and whose history I could only imagine. Meanwhile my father became acquainted with descendants of the colonists and their unique past. Now in narrative detail and with a wealth of photographs, the story of Aurora belongs to all of us.

—JOHN SHERRILL HOUSER, international sculptor

The colonists loved color, painting chairs red, blue, and yellow, and quilting their petticoats in blends of colorful prints and plaids. They even painted the washtubs blue. Notice the Tumbling Block quilt. *ACHS photo*

Introduction

The story of the Aurora Colony might be considered a story of craftsmanship as much as anything else. It is the crafted items that survive with the greatest testimony to the skill and the commitment of the workers who made up Dr. Keil's communal society.

Wilhelm Keil held the fundamental truth of Christianity to be "love one another" and the Diamond Rule: to make another's life better than one's own. As Charles Nordhoff wrote in 1874, "the value of united action, the value to each of the example of others, the comfort of social ties, and the security against absolute poverty and helplessness, amounts to a great deal."

The colonists had the advantage, however, of bringing their skills to the table, providing furniture, baskets, metal products, and textiles to the other members of the community. They worked on necessary projects together, whether it was the building of homes, the church, the hotel—or the clearing of land or the harvesting of the fruit crop. When it was time to pick apples, the shoemaker assisted with the picking of apples.

This attention to task with patient energy and perseverance, united in harmonious cooperation, helped the colonists achieve a large measure of security and independence. Each member had a special knack for a particular skill or task, and by common consent the members recognized the best craftspeople among them.

The Aurora Colony spirit manifested best in commitment to work and craft. The language to describe this process will rarely be found in their writings but is illustrated in their surviving artifacts—the quilt, the basket, the chair. The colonists, all descendants of old-world craftsmen, appreciated the relationship of color and form, and they made beautiful objects that were meant to be used. The finished products are remarkable for their simplicity.

We gather a portion of those artifacts through photographs and narrative to remember their stories and, through them, to let their craft inspire our own.

—PATRICK J. HARRIS, curator, Aurora Colony Historical Society

The colonists designed stencils like this one for use on furniture and walls.

A colony-made wheel of the Wolfer family commemorates the second migration of colonists from Bethel, Missouri, to Aurora, Oregon. A bolt fit into the square opening above the round hub to secure the wheel to its wagon. The Double Irish Chain quilt, 1863, maker unknown, is cotton with a handquilted feather wreath design, eight stitches per inch. (85 x 87.5 inches; ACHS collection.) *JK photo*

Detail from Double Irish Chain

Craft

Past and Present Intertwined

Craft…is our identity and our legacy.
—former president JIMMY CARTER,
Craft in America

In Oregon's verdant Willamette Valley there once lived a cluster of German Americans seeking something more, something splendid and essential at both spiritual and temporal levels. They found it in their Christian communal society, established in the mid–nineteenth century, one of the only successful such communities in the West.

Not unlike the Amana Society of Iowa or the Harmonists of Pennsylvania, the Aurora colonists expressed their values and traditions through interactions with the world around them. At a time in the twenty-first century when people are often disconnected from the work of their hands, from neighbors, extended family, and faith, these colonists demonstrated who

Tumbling Blocks, circa 1860–70, 66 x 84 inches, maker unknown

William Keil, the former tailor-turned-herbalist, self-trained preacher, and colony leader named his Bethel, Missouri, home Elim—perhaps after the desert oasis of Old Testament accounts (see Exodus 15:27 and Numbers 33:9) where the Israelites camped in exodus from Egypt. Keil replicated the house, using lumber instead of brick, in Aurora, the utopian community of his dreams. *ACHS photo*

they were by their unique crafts and traditions, food, music, furniture, and fiber arts—and by living out their beliefs within community. They passed down their stories, one generation to the next, not through many written accounts but through quilts, crafts, and traditions—the works of their hands are their voices.

The artifacts left behind are preserved inside the properties owned by the Aurora Colony Historical Society at the Old Aurora Colony Museum and the Stauffer-Will farmstead near the present-day village of Aurora, Oregon. Additional quilts are owned privately and often shared for exhibits. Aurora is Oregon's most unique National Historic District, where the society has preserved nearly one hundred quilts and textiles as well as baskets, furniture, tools of tin and wood, and other artifacts, all connected with the colony period (1856–83). They're showcased in facilities owned by the historical society, including an 1862 oxbarn, an 1865 farmhouse, an 1876 log cabin, and a family home built in the 1860s and lived in until 1967. These artifacts, housed in colorful period exhibits, act as signatures and reflect the simple passions of a faithful people.

We are privileged more than a century and a half later to experience a part of their lives in our contemporary world and consider how we are bound with them through threads of art, community, faith, and healing, the past and present intertwined.

The Legacy Continues

Today, the fiber arts and craftsmanship of these early colonists are celebrated with living-history programs that engage children in the work of one's hands. Each spring, fourth graders from neighboring schools bake biscuits in the old stove at the Stauffer-Will farmhouse. In the upstairs bedroom of the farmhouse, they sit on colony rugs and piece together swatches of cloth to form blocks and hear of quilting while the sun shines through wavy handblown windows against a handturned spool bed covered with a colorful quilt. They pull rough yarn with little fingers as a volunteer spins the wool, surprised that socks or scarves come from grazing sheep. In the barn,

they cut a branch they'll drill a hole in for the hand-dipped candle they'll make and take home. They split shingles and put their names on them to cover holes in the chicken-coop roof. They individualize their own crafts and do it as a part of a community, making a memory of the experience.

Adults also participate both as volunteers and as guests of the society during Strawberry Socials (June), Aurora Colony Days (August), and living-history tours at structures maintained by the society. When the rainy season arrives, several colony homes still lived in are graciously opened for a holiday tour where quilts and other textiles are displayed. Volunteers produce a candlelight drama every year at Christmas, serving apple cider and cookies made with colony tin cutters. This celebration is reminiscent perhaps of that Christ Day promenade where little girls placed candles in tin stars on the colony tree. The old ways are witnessed to with stories, food is served in order to restore the spirit, and musicians provide background music.

The colony's musical legacy is continued as volunteers and staff restore original colony orchestral arrangements and band music acquired by the society in 2002 and delivered "in three cardboard boxes containing 175

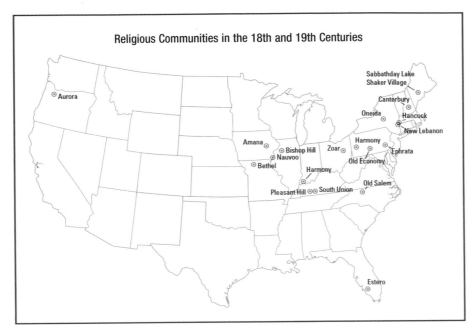

Religious Communities in the 18th and 19th Centuries

Sabbathday Lake Shaker Village

Canterbury

Oneida   Hancock

Aurora   New Lebanon

Amana   Harmony
    Bishop Hill   Zoar   Ephrata
    Nauvoo   Old Economy
    Bethel   Harmony

                                          Old Salem
Pleasant Hill   South Union

                                          Estero

Of all the religious communal societies begun in the nineteenth century, only Aurora survived in the West.

moldy, damp and deteriorating nineteenth-century books and folios." The owner of these treasures was Lloyd Mills, who inherited the items from his parents and several successive owners of an Aurora home (once occupied by colonist physician and pharmacist Martin Giesy). The compositions survived a fire and the ravages of time; Dr. Keil Richards, PhD, professor emeritus at Lewis and Clark College of Oregon, called the material "the most significant find in my seventy years of music."[1]

Written with crow-quill pens in now-faded blackberry juice ink, a Portland State University instructor, Andrew Willette, is authenticating the pieces, digitalizing them and making them available to thousands of school children for use in performances. In 2008, more than three hundred CDs containing audio performances and some musical compositions were mailed to schools around Oregon for students to learn to play history for themselves—just in time to help celebrate Oregon's one hundred and fiftieth anniversary of statehood in 2009.

Throughout the year, the museum itself provides rotating exhibits celebrating color, family stories, historical periods, and craft. Three novels based on the life of one of the colonists, Emma Wagner Giesy; Eugene Snyder's book *Aurora, Their Last Utopia: Oregon's Christian Commune 1856–1883;* the Aurora colony *Heritage Recipes;* and CDs of music of the Aurora Colony Band are available for sale in the colony gift store along with cookie cutters, cross-stitch kits, and patterns for prairie dolls.

Women in Aurora continue to quilt. Every Tuesday they gather to stitch a quilt top someone has brought. Others quilt winning blocks for an annual contest; these quilts are raffled off to help fund this fully self-sustaining museum.

Perhaps the greatest event is held each October: the Aurora Quilt Show. Begun more than thirty-five years ago, before many communities recognized the artistry and craftsmanship of quilting, the show displays some of the original colony quilts, textiles, and clothing within the society's collection. Frequently, privately held colony quilts are included along with handmade garments, coverlets, other textiles, baskets, and metalwork made by colonists.

Colorful exhibits display musical instruments, the famous *Schellenbaum* that led the way west, miniature doll houses, toys, and blue-painted trunks

Ocean Waves, quilter unknown, graces colony pews from 1867, now part of the Aurora Presbyterian Church. It includes handpieced cotton shirting, solids, geometric prints, and double pink calico, with quilting in small, even stitches. (77 x 80 inches; ACHS collection.) *JK photo*

associated with the colony's history. The displays are exhibited throughout the Oxbarn Museum, the Steinbach cabin, and on both floors of the Giesy-Kraus House next door.

For ten days each fall, people can examine these textile treasures and handcrafted artifacts of the men and women who followed God, a man, and a dream and crossed a continent to live a spare and splendid life within community. A slow walk through the exhibits reminds us of the healing beauty that arises out of quilts and crafts made with loving care.

As during the colony period, all are welcome.

Wrapped in Art, Crafts, and Beauty

I began seeing quilts and crafts as stories while wandering through antique stores imagining how people once used a strange-looking tool or how many hours it took to piece a now-worn Ocean Waves quilt. Then several of my novels were chosen to be quilted by various quilting groups in the Northwest. The beauty and uniqueness of these fiber stories made me more conscious of quilts as narratives and how such crafts reflected the women who had made them. My interest was cemented a few years later when I was invited to be the guest scholar for a weekend retreat of quilters led by quilter and writer Mary Bywater Cross. Even though I'd never quilted, she asked me to speak of stories and how they informed our lives. While I told stories, the women from around the country sewed and stitched, having brought their material and machines with them to the Willamette Valley.

During a break, I paged through Mary's book *Quilts of the Oregon Trail* and there found a story of a quilt stitched by Emma Wagner Giesy. Her story, and that of the colonies she came from, led me to Aurora and its roots in Germany; then to Indiana, Pennsylvania, Missouri, Washington State, and finally Oregon. Emma's fiber art served as her legacy. The Change and Cherish Historical Series (WaterBrook Multnomah Publishing Group) chronicles her journey to celebrate her voice in a larger society that often acted tone-deaf to its female members.

In the process of researching and writing, I fell in love with the way the community stumbled and righted itself as it chose to carry out its faith in an everyday world. And it is my hope, and that of the Aurora Colony Historical Society, that telling their stories and the stories of these treasures will inspire the reader's own exploration of family,

legacy, and community. These artifacts allow us a new look at the crafts that enrich our lives and help memorialize the triumphs and tragedies of our ancestors. Join me on this journey to another place and time. We'll explore the landscapes, relationships, work, and faith—the building blocks of community. And we'll see how a band of German Americans wished to live a simple, meaningful life in the American West, and how the work of their hands brings comfort.

The original oxbarn colonists built in Aurora in 1862 now houses portions of the Old Aurora Colony Museum.
JC photo

Landscapes

Where They Came From, Where They Headed

I would describe myself
like a landscape I've studied
at length, in detail;
like a word I'm coming to understand.
—RAINER MARIA RILKE, *Rilke's Book
of Hours: Love Poems to God*

A quilt most likely lay across the oak casket, a pieced fan pattern or maybe Running Squares. Pieces of mourning cloth and wools as dark as walnut bark, likely pieced by the colonists to wrap in as they journeyed west, instead were spread to honor the deceased and comfort the grieving. In front of the casket, a sturdy boy or young man carried the *Schellenbaum,* a German musical instrument with a dozen tiny tinkling bells, arcing to the sky on a brass standard like a flag.

Matilda Knight Stauffer's Sunflower, circa 1867, 84 x 97 inches

The women finished loading tightly woven oak and ash baskets onto the backs of green-painted wagons built by the colonists themselves. Then they packed the blue and red coverlets, handwoven. Next, like mother hens, they gathered up their families and prepared to say last good-byes to parents, uncles, aunts, and even older children. A portion of this colony of German Americans would soon head west from Bethel's brick buildings and the copses of spring-bud maples and hickory, following the fringe-covered hearse.

Trumpets sounded, the clink of harness and hames accompanying the announcement of their departure. A poem composed by the father was sung, a funeral dirge. In the background, one heard the chatter of children laughing—for who can keep a child from finding joy in a new journey even with death riding beside?

It was 1855. The Bethelites, as they were known, were members of a Christian communal utopian society, inspired by the words in the second chapter of the book of Acts, about gathering their gifts and talents into a common fund from which all needs would be met.

Service. Brotherhood. Compassion. These concepts drove many groups to experiment with communal living in the early 1800s, a response to the northern European struggles and discontent of the 1700s. Stringent religious beliefs and rituals had caused thousands to rebel and poured emigrants onto the American landscape. Distinctive groups spilled out of the melting pot of struggle: Pietists, Hutterites, Inspirationists, Shakers.[1] Some saw communal living as a way to live closer to

Detail from the Sunflower quilt shows its handpieced back in a variety of cotton fabric scraps. *JK photo*

God's Word, even to prepare for the Second Coming. Others were experimenters often following strong, charismatic leaders who promised the joys of heaven on earth or a place of refuge in a time of threatening wars and social unrest.

Dr. Heinrich Wilhelm (the German version of the English William) Keil began his ministerial career as an Evangelical Methodist Christian, though his views changed along with the new landscapes he sought and settled on, his moves taking him from Prussia to New York, then Pittsburgh, then Bethel, Missouri. One hundred people formed his vanguard.

In 1853, two years before the departure of the mournful wagon train, a scouting party of nine men and one woman had been sent out from Bethel by their leader, Dr. Keil (as he liked to be called), to find a new site for their colony. Three criteria were required:

1. An isolated landscape to allow pursuit of their communal ways by living close to the land in service to their faith—and to remove them from the struggles of a civil war already visible on the horizon

2. Stands of timber, found by scouts, for the many homes they'd need when the bulk of the Bethelites came west

3. Farmland close enough to markets for, through their crops and what they manufactured, the colonists hoped to replicate their success in Missouri of meeting all their own needs and selling goods to neighbors

Returning scouts had sung the praises of the Washington Territory found in late 1853, and in May 1855 the Bethel colonists prepared to reach it, fulfilling their hopes for new beginnings.

Then just days before the departure, a son died. The father directed that he be carried west and, with his eight siblings, make the journey with the Keil family. The treasured cargo carried in that casket from Bethel, Missouri, across the continent, was Willie, son of Wilhelm (though he seldom used his first name) and Louisa Keil. Willie's father, the utopian community's charismatic leader, had since the 1840s stitched his flock together with tight threads. Trained as a tailor, self-taught in the herbal arts, Keil gathered up former Evangelicals and Lutherans from George Rapp's shattered communal Pennsylvania society, and wooed separatists disillusioned by yet another charismatic leader, Count Leon (who had broken from Rapp himself and formed his own version of how Christians should live). Keil had shown in Missouri how it could be done successfully. Now like thousands of other Americans,

they headed west, taking their community and craftsmanship with them.

"There were a right goodly number of men in the colony adept in the crafts, such as ironsmiths, carpenters, cobblers, weavers, cabinet-makers, and volunteers from these craftsmen made up the major portion of the personnel of the first Keil emigration train to the great Oregon Country."[2] Many of these men descended from European guilds known for their individuality of creation and their quality of production. What they could not bring with them due to space limitations, they could be quite certain they could reproduce once they arrived.

The father had delayed the start while colonists built that covered, tin-lined casket and filled it with the colony's own Golden Rule Whiskey and the son's body. Willie would be buried in the West, where colony scouts awaited the arrival of nearly two hundred members of this unique communal group.

Why Wilhelm Keil chose to take his son west rather than bury him in Missouri is uncertain. Perhaps he decried

The Bethel-made *Schellenbaum,* always carried first in colonists' processions, led the way to Aurora. For musical performances, the *Schellenbaum* was lifted up, then its stand struck on the floor to jingle the many bells. *ACHS photo*

the fevers in Missouri that the colonists suffered with each year, fevers that in 1855 had taken his oldest son's life. Perhaps grief convinced him to keep the boy with him yet a little longer. Maybe Louisa Keil, his wife, wanted her oldest son buried close to where the colony would establish its new community. It's even likely that as the leader, Keil felt adamant about keeping his promise to his son that he would ride in the lead wagon, seeing the journey as a way to memorialize for the colonists the idea that anything can be accomplished with faith, fortitude, and ingenuity.

The group seemed blessed with good food, music, and a trouble-free crossing. They hardly lost an ox or had to patch a pair of pants, or so they said later in letters written along the way. The changing landscapes marveled some: rugged rocks and snow-capped mountains piercing an otherwise flat plain. Massive river gorges promised challenge along with opportunity. The colonists celebrated each time they successfully forded streams or encountered Indian people who assisted rather than attacked. A violin might serenade a campfire; sometimes an impromptu dance would follow.

Other settlers encountered along the trail sometimes asked to join their journey. Their wagons held together well. They'd prepared and packed lightly, knowing when they arrived they'd reproduce their *Kleiderschränke* (large wardrobes), looms, and lathes.

Mornings, they set aside their pretzels and brown breads, choosing zwieback prepared before they'd left to save time from baking. They organized at nooning and

This Redwork square, "A Promise Kept," from a contemporary cotton quilt originally designed by Janus Childs, depicts the historic departure from Bethel, Willie Keil's casket in the lead. (70 x 72 inches; private collection.) *NL photo*

Dr. Wilhelm Keil in later Aurora days. *ACHS photo*

Dr. Keil's 1860's Aurora home. He built a similar house for his son and daughter-in-law, Frederick and Louisa Giesy, where the fine craftsmanship (as in handturned porch pillars) is evident, but the lack of convenience baffling. The kitchen was in the basement, requiring Louisa to carry food up and down two stairways for meals in the dining room or to feed sick family members in bedrooms on the third floor. *ACHS photo*

efficiently circled their stock inside the corral of wagons each night. Keil wrote of local Indian people riding in to join their campfires, exchanging fresh game for colony-made homespun shirts and peering with curiosity at the casket carrying Keil's son. Along the route, imagine women relieved by an occasional rest, airing out quilts made damp by sudden prairie storms or baking strudels with dried fruit brought from Missouri. There was little time to piece quilts, though some women cross-stitched as they walked or leaned down to help unroll the samplers on which their daughters worked. Then at night, they wrapped themselves in functional Nine Patch bedsacks, a foreshadowing of modern sleeping bags.

Despite the fact the colonists carried with them a mournful hearse, more than funeral dirges accompanied the group. Music, most written with a crow-quill pen dipped in blackberry juice, brought festivity and healing through cornets, clarinets, and German-manufactured brass instruments. They let music remind them of the landscape they had left, and later, when they told of their journey, the music brought back memories of the mountains and prairies they'd crossed.

Carving a People

A small portion of Keil's overland group arrived in the rainforest of western Washington Territory in a rainy October 1855. Within weeks, Keil buried his son on a hill overlooking the Willapa River in Pacific County. A gravestone marks the site off Highway 6 in western Washington State. But here the letters back to Bethel change tone, describing a foreboding landscape of dense trees, rain, and mud. Firs reached such heights a man could fall over seeking to see the tops, and forest duff beneath, dank and dark, made walking treacherous. Keil wrote,

> The land itself cannot be excelled anywhere in the world in fertility and productivity, for everything one plants grows luxuriantly and abundantly. But nobody knows what to do with the things he produces.... There is no market for the things produced;...there is no prospect for the develop-

ment of such market;...everything that one needs is too far away and too expensive.... To clear the forest is so expensive that I would not undertake to clear and fence a single acre for less than $100. It would be impossible to produce our own clothing here. There are no sheep in these parts; to bring them here would be expensive, and even if they were here, there would be no fodder to feed them. Carding machines and looms cannot be established here unless the wool be imported from California or South America. Neither could tanneries be established.... If I should wish to found for ourselves a home in this valley such as we had in Missouri, the initial expense would not be less than $100,000, for there is too little open land and the clearing of the dense forest is too difficult.[3]

He sent word that those following should turn back and winter in Portland. The Willapa landscape, though beautiful and Eden-like in summer, had thorns in winter: unrelenting wind, rain, and swollen rivers that carved the forest landscape. The timber rose so massively that scouts could not use the tools they had to fell and notch logs for houses. Their work went slowly—too slowly for Keil. As the Bethelites endured the winter in Willapa, their leader saw few opportunities for enough production to feed and clothe his flock even if there'd been structures enough to serve the immigrants. The scouts and their families lived clustered together in a stockade they'd built along with a few log huts with canvas roofs. They barely survived on salmon and old potatoes and gifts of roots and berries from local natives.

In early 1856, with some disdain for their having chosen so poor a site, Keil said good-bye to the scouts who'd spent two years attempting to harness the landscape—including Emma Wagner Giesy and her husband, Christian—and joined those spending the winter in Portland, Oregon.

Handwoven in 1840 by A. Horr of Harmony, Pennsylvania, this red, navy, and cream reversible coverlet traveled the Oregon Trail. Woven into one corner is the name *Schuele* (an Aurora colonist), who was likely the person who commissioned the work. Fringed on three sides, the border features five-inch birds and a tree, with blocks of stars and flowers at the center. (72 x 90.5 inches; ACHS collection.) *NL photo*

In the frontier town of Portland, the colonists spread out, asking for refuge in the homes of settlers, working in return for food and shelter. Keil put his herbal medicinal skills to work, trading for food and necessities. Women washed and ironed clothes for Portland's finest. And from their crowded clapboard rental, Keil sought a site for his now-scattered colony.

By spring, he located a prairie south of the emerging town of Portland, where the landscape offered greater hope of the colonists' successful venture. Keil called the property Aurora Mills after his young daughter, Aurora. Along with prairie land, bordered by more manageable timber and some hardwoods, Aurora Mills "lay almost hidden in the timber-covered lower Willamette Valley, near the junction of several prairie streams and a dashing, rock bottom, mountain stream," not far above the falls of the Willamette River and the curve of the Pudding River.[4] The waterways were ideal for product transport and close to growing cities like Oregon City, Portland, and Salem.

Here, Keil found his hope.

Several colonists composed music and used materials at hand: blackberry juice ink and a crow's quill pen. *ACHS photo*

Building a Community

Keil chose 320 acres along a much-traveled road used by aging fur trappers, those heading to the California gold mines and back, and newly arriving settlers seeking their own landscapes, facts that proved providential for their success. Keil might well have said such success was all about location, location, location, but industry helped too. A grist and lumber mill already operated on the site, and Keil purchased them as well.

Carving a farm took endurance and teamwork. Whether these colonists are at an early building site (some property was assigned away from Aurora proper) or on a brief camping respite is not known. *ACHS photo*

From Portland, he sent a small contingent of men and one woman to begin building. We don't know the woman's name, but we assume she cooked for the men who logged trees and cleared ground for crops; perhaps she left her mark through a special recipe or how many berries she gathered in the baskets she brought.

It was said that as the colonists began building, teams of four men each were required to fell a tree before breakfast or, if low on meat, bring in a deer for the woman to cook.[5] The first structure built by the colonists was a log home for the workers, followed by *Das Grosse Haus,* or The Big House, designed for Dr. Keil and his family. Bachelors populated its upper loft. In a few years, a larger two-and-a-half-story structure, sash-sawed of local materials in a typical Aurora design, rose up at the top of the hill as a new *Grosse Haus.* It had a wide center hallway and staircase flanked by large rooms; working bachelors once again took over the attic.

A communal wash house or summer kitchen and smokehouses likely went up next. The colonists built a big, Pennsylvania-style blue-painted horse barn and an oxbarn, much to the surprise of their Willamette Valley neighbors. The usually mild winters, in comparison to those of Missouri and Pennsylvania, allowed farmers in this Northwest to leave their animals outside, beneath large cedar trees in soft December rains. Regardless, the colonists sought protection for their animals. Though today the blue barn is gone, the oxbarn still stands as home of the Old Aurora Colony Museum.

From *Das Grosse Haus,* Keil directed the building of his communal society, and new structures dotted the swales and dips toward springs and rivers, like eggs clustered in an ever-widening nest. Framed houses rose slowly as colonists were sent to work outside Aurora, earning salaries they returned to help build the colony coffers so Keil could purchase needed goods that colonists could not raise or make themselves.

At first they sold lumber to surrounding settlers rather than build their own houses. Keil often sent men to help others fell oak in return for the bark that was of more use in the tanning process for hides—which the colonists planned to later convert into leather—than for fuel or lumber. So those first winters, large numbers of colony families continued to cluster together, foregoing their usual single-family homes.

Later, most colony structures were constructed of fir or cedar that the land reluctantly gave up; these structures rose to two-and-a-half stories, usually rectangular with a single chimney and often a central staircase instead of the traditional stairwell rising at one end. Log homes also dotted the community, known by colonists as simply Aurora, a Latin word meaning "dawn." The colony didn't officially drop *Mills* until it incorporated in 1893.

In the midst of building, Wilhelm Keil worried over the management of events back in Bethel. Land there needed to be sold and more craftsmen start west; but these transactions were awkward with all the property in Bethel listed in Keil's name only. At various times he appears to have wondered at the magnitude of his own choices. One winter, he advised the Bethelites not to sell at all as things were so miserable and uncertain in the new locale.

Then spring returned with its lush cornucopia of promise, and the land itself appeared to bless all efforts. Keil had purchased apple starts near Fort Vancouver when they'd first arrived in 1855; the colonists planted orchards in felled-timber areas. Before the trees could produce, they purchased apples at a dollar a bushel from neighbors, sliced and dried the apples for their own use, then saved the peels to make apple cider sold back to those same neighbors for a dollar and a half a gallon—an early sign of both inventiveness and commercial acumen in their new land.

Colony women set out herbs whose plants were likely carried in paper cones across the plains. Primarily used for medicinal purposes, herbs also flavored foods that would later spread their fame, added fragrance when folded into clothing, and were drunk as teas on wet winter nights.

The landscape gave up its treasures in the seasons: Wheat grew well and was ground at the colony mill. Berries ripened and were dried. Game still ranged close. Colonists occasionally had mutton and butchered hogs. Much later, they planted hops both for beer the colonists made and sold and for hops packs used for healing and cooking. Oregon grapes grew wild for wines made "strongly medicinal," or so reads the 1861 State Agricultural Society's announcement in the *Weekly Oregonian,* granting the award to Dr. Keil. Where Indian people once burned brush on the prairie, colonists now found good fodder for their cattle and sheep, fostering the ability to produce wool for their own garments and to tailor clothing for neighbors.

A former tailor, Keil knew what seamstresses required, so some of the earliest entries on the communal store's ledger books are for thread and calico, both imported materials. While many of the women's dresses used calico or linen in dark colors, their aprons shown bright white, and beneath somber dresses they wore pieced petticoats, richly hemmed with vibrant colors, even red. The colonists made all their own clothing from plaids woven at the colony mill, including home-sewn quilted capes splashed with color. Surrounding settlers began making their way to Aurora, which neighboring villages referred to as Dutchtown, for well-tailored garments. Newspaper accounts praise the colonists as the best-dressed people in the Willamette Valley.

Later, leather goods like fine shoes, harnesses and saddles, and milliners' wares were purchased in Aurora… but not before Keil's pleas to bring new recruits and artisans from Bethel were finally answered.

Ye shall go out with joy, and be led forth with peace: the mountains and the hills shall break forth before you into singing, and all the trees of the field shall clap their hands.

—ISAIAH 55:12, ABS

A Time to Create

The artisans crafted from local woods lathes to create distinctive furniture and crafts, and looms used to form fine linen into cloth and coverlets as well as yarns into sturdy yet eye-soothing rugs. They constructed spinning wheels, including a special one that had an oscillating arm, allowing the spinner to sit while making the arm move back and forth—and this variation on the more typical walking wheel dramatically increased production. They made tools to tighten their rope beds, fashioned an apple corer out of tin, and wove arm cuffs out of straw to protect their sleeves when picking berries or harvesting hay. They traded their work for pottery used for storing beans and salted pork. And eventually there were enough hands and help that the women could return to piecing quilts.

Colonists' relationships with their land and one another inspired quilt patterns with landscape themes and nature-inspired names: Bay Leaf, Bear Paw, Grape Basket. Ocean Waves was a popular choice, perhaps quilted in remembrance of those colonists who remained in the Willapa country where oysters were farmed like fields. A quilt called Sunflower, made by Matilda Knight Stauffer, who spent time in the ocean country of Willapa, shows a seashell scallop as part of the quilting, unique to the colony's more traditional double-stitched wreath quilting. Birds

The first scouts sent west in 1853 chose an isolated, forbidding, heavily treed and rained-upon landscape in Washington Territory. Here, the Stauffer family and friends commemorate their first years in Willapa. *ACHS photo*

The feather wreath quilting on Old Maid's Puzzle, quilter unknown, is a common indicator of Aurora Colony design. The handpieced cotton quilt features diagonal quilting on a 7.5-inch pink border. Subtly quilted within the wreath are the letters *S* and *W,* perhaps providing a clue to its maker. (Circa 1875–90; 87 x 71 inches; ACHS collection.) Also pictured is the log and brick foundation work of the Stauffer-Will farmhouse. *JK photo*

were a common theme. Pin Wheel commemorated spring winds, and a hexagon pattern was surely reminiscent of the blooms grown back East.

The colonists dyed their own yarn, bleaching it until the water was a murky hue, signaling the readiness to accept color. Later a designated dyeing specialist led these efforts. In time, they mastered bright colors of Turkey red, blue, and purple, and dark colors like black and navy. Alum was the mordant most used to make the colors fast. Boiled peach leaves created a perfect green, madder root the deeper reds. Walnut hulls turned yarn brown, and boiled onion skins formed yellows. A color wheel like one found in an 1869 schoolbook reminded them of hues they wished to master.

Colony Easter eggs were colored "pink, orange, lavender, lilac, purple, maroon, rust, fuchsia, red, brown and varying tints of green."[6] One could expect those same dyes to make their way into the rugs and other fiber crafts that consumed the Aurora women's time and interests when they weren't producing essentials.

Eventually new resources and craftsmen came into the fold. In 1862, Henry C. Finck, Bethel's music director, arrived with his five children by ship through Panama, taking advantage of the Panama Railroad running across that isthmus, avoiding both the long journey around the South American horn and the trials of an overland trek. He'd married a daughter of a colonist who died before their journey west. While Finck never became an official member, he contributed greatly to the life of the community through his university education and musical expertise. He led the Aurora band and the choruses that initially included separate men's and women's groups and eventually a mixed chorus. In some ways, "Professor" Finck represented the blend of relationships found in the colony, with nonmembers actively intertwined in the lives of the colonists as well as engaging with the neighboring communities of Portland, Needy, Barlow, and later, Canby.

By the mid-1860s almost all of the original scouts and families who had remained in Willapa, where Willie Keil was buried, had moved to Aurora, and Bethelites migrated to Aurora in 1863, 1865, and 1867, both overland and by sea. Keil sought to purchase more property to accommodate the new arrivals, and some began farming land several miles from Aurora proper. These people still considered themselves members of the Aurora Colony, and most are buried in the community cemetery that bears the town's name.

In 1863, a group led by Christopher Wolff brought new life and insights. Wolff, a graduate of the University of Göttingen, had been one of the principals in charge at Bethel. At Aurora, he provided tutoring beyond the primary level and taught classes of adults in the evenings on physics, geography, Greek, and Latin.[7] He remained a Lutheran throughout his life, as did Karl Ruge, another university-educated teacher, and one can speculate that the theology of these men along with the musical genius of Henry C. Finck influenced the worship of the colonists. Their presence, held in high regard, also attests to Keil's willingness to tolerate religious differences within his flock.

John Vogt led eleven, Missouri mule-drawn wagons carrying sixty people to Aurora in 1865. But the 1867 group of George Link marked the end of the mass migrations. Aurora counted then six hundred in the colony, its size not much different from today's population, though the population fluctuated with migrations streaming in and colonists traveling out for brief times. People traveled east to visit friends in Economy and Phillipsburg, Penn-

sylvania. August Keil, one of Wilhelm and Louisa's sons, traveled back to help manage affairs in Bethel.

Little in Aurora resembled the well-laid-out, mature community of Bethel these industrious colonists had left behind. Because of the slope and dips of the land and to maximize the existing stage-line trail, the streets of Aurora weren't localized around a central square. Mill ponds, timber stands, and deep ravines rose up from streams to break up the town so much that in 1863, when Bethelite George Wolfer arrived, he asked a man he'd known at Bethel, "How far is it to Aurora?" and Henry Fry replied, "You are *in* Aurora."

"This so took the wind out of my sails," Wolfer wrote, "that I was speechless."[8]

Eventually, the colonists constructed Park House, set high on a hill amid the trees and where they hosted strawberry festivals and other gatherings. Music serenaded visitors as they wandered through the paths and down the ravines to the town proper. Those with history of George

Though I cannot see the gentle waves pushing across the shoals on Willapa Bay,
I know the tide line by the sound.... I know the sea is there and in the daylight I will find it
once again but it will look so different. This is the promise of a night walk on the beach.

—*A Tendering in the Storm*

Joseph Resch ran Boones Ferry on the Willamette River, which the colonists used to transport their goods and interact with outsiders. Members of the Muessig family shown here eventually intermarried with the Keil family. *ACHS photo*

Rapp's society of the early 1800s, from which families such as the Wagners, Forstners, Wolfers, and others separated, would recall the labyrinths of those Pennsylvania gardens and likely reproduced them in Aurora.

Looking east, one could see Mount Hood with its glacier shining white the summer through and view the shake roofs of houses as the village loosened its tight belt through the years, expanding east and south of Mill Dam.

It was in the village proper where the Keil and Company Store kept track of trade, and not far away stood Dr. Martin Giesy's pharmacy where he treated patients and dispensed apothecary cures to colonists and neighboring residents alike. A separate store permitted neighbors to purchase items using cash, while the colony store relied on account books crediting labor performed and resources received against what was taken by colony members to meet needs. In the beginning, only one woman had her name on a ledger page: Emma Giesy, wife of the scout who had led the group west to Washington Territory and who was known as a fine seamstress. Later, ledgers began to show other women's purchases individualized and not just on pages of their husbands, brothers, fathers, or sons.

The colony's hotel stood a short distance above Mill Dam; the three-story construction eventually became a train stop and featured a platform on top, where the Aurora band played to welcome new arrivals. Here the colonists met the outside world and fed them well, becoming known from Victoria to San Francisco for their culinary arts. The train might have gone on into Portland—the city was but twenty miles ahead—but the tracks made their way along the old stage route, and the scents of sausage and fresh bread dinners stopped passengers at Aurora first.

A Time to Change

In 1872, Keil began issuing title of property to individuals rather than keeping all in his name. Perhaps this was at the urging of the young people, many of whom were drawn to the capitalist economy of the young Oregon state. Upon Keil's death in 1877, the colony began the process of disbanding, and the properties in Bethel and

Aurora were dispersed to registered members, the final dissolution occurring in 1883.

All around them the landscape shaped the work and progress of the colonists, affecting who they interacted with, how their work and faith were nurtured, and how they found their new beginnings. The word *landscape* derives from Dutch painters describing aspects of an interior. The Aurora landscape today continues to frame the interior of this communal experiment of an earlier era and the arts and crafts that came to symbolize its journey.

The Wagner family used this brass candlestick to light evenings along the Oregon Trail. The Wagners journeyed from Bethel, Missouri, in 1862 to join their daughter Emma Wagner Giesy in Aurora, Oregon. (Private collection.) *JK photo*

Colonists hired local Indian people to assist with harvests. Notice the children who came to work alongside parents, as well as the ease between two different American cultures. *ACHS photo*

Relationships

"Who is My Neighbor?"

I wish I could make you understand what a peaceful,
industrious and harmonious group of people composed
the Aurora Colony. We all had what we needed, we all
worked, and we were all one family.

—Elizabeth Giesy, colony member

Unlike some communal societies that foster isolation, Aurora colonists spent time with their neighbors. Along the journey west, it's said that Keil's daughter, Aurora, was especially popular with the Indian people and they gave her trinkets she might have worn or placed around a prairie doll's neck.

In Oregon, the colonists often employed Indian people to help pick fruit or hops and tend sheep, but their nearest contacts were not natives as some stories of western settlement suggest. By the time Methodist missionaries made their first

Aurora Keil's Appliquéd Birds on Wool, circa 1890–1910, 60 x 46 inches

Aurora Keil, age twelve, for whom the colony was named, died of smallpox along with three of her siblings in the weeks before Christmas 1862. The senior Keils would outlive all but three of their nine children, Dr. Keil's remedies unable to forestall their early deaths. *ACHS photo*

forays into the region in the 1830s, most of the Kalapuya people, who had gathered, hunted, and burned brush to create meadows that would lure deer and elk, had vanished. A few children and old people survived, though not enough to remember the native names for creeks and hilltops as did the longer-surviving tribes in the Washington Territory. Most tribes in the Oregon country had been removed to reservations by the treaties of 1855 or decimated by diseases carried on board ships entering the Columbia River. For years both native and nonnative who lived in the lower, sometime-swampy climes of the Willamette Valley suffered from the agues, fevers that must have reminded the colonists of those suffering times in Missouri.

Many of Keil's colonists learned English, facilitating trade connections with other settlers and retired French Canadian fur trappers; they exchanged butter for cotton cloth or Buena Vista pottery, goods they did not make themselves. As early as 1857, neighbors made purchases from the Keil and Company Store, and colonists helped them build or clear fields.

As the colony grew, so did the outsiders who came to Aurora for finely tailored clothes, shoes, and other products that carried with them the guarantee of superior workmanship. Occasionally a young colonist might meet someone from the outside, perhaps at the Agricultural Fair or at an Aurora band concert. Mostly, colonists intermarried with long-time followers of Keil, who approved—or disapproved—all potential nuptials.

This mix of colony outreach and acceptance of gradient levels of noncolonist involvement appears to be a hallmark of this communal group and contributed to long-lasting status within the Oregon country. In fact, what the colonists presented to the outside world, through their music, food, craftsmanship, and offers of assistance, is the purest demonstration of their Christian values and beliefs. They accepted those who did not share their faith but who still honored their community values. They traded fairly their finest work and offered help and compassion to outsiders. And they acted out the answer to the biblical question, "What does the LORD require of you? To act justly and to love mercy and to walk humbly with your God" (Micah 6:8).

They were made up of large families. In later years, Keil did not discourage celibacy, and in some instances he forbade marriages not so much from policy as his objecting to the matches. But weddings were festive occasions and gatherings. Special clothing made for the celebrations included men's and boy's suits and, of course, wedding dresses.

Christina Kocher, a colony member, stitched a wedding dress she never wore because of Keil's refusal to sanction the marriage. Her relatives must have been concerned, as they wrote to a colony member in 1868, "We do not understand the marriage policy especially in view of the fact your children are of age and none of them are married. Could the reason be a religious one, or a family one?"[1]

Christina Kocher never wore this purple taffeta and satin, two-piece wedding dress because Dr. Keil, for no known reason, would not approve her marriage to Israel Snyder. Skilled tailoring includes a vertically pleated hemline of the underskirt and at the neck, draping of the overskirt across the front, a stylish bustle in the back, and an intricately shirred and ruched bodice. (Private collection.) *JK photo*

Colonists prepare to picnic with a colony-made basket, a tied utility quilt in the arms of the father. As usual, the family dog joins the outing. *ACHS photo*

Russell Blankenship, writing in the mid-twentieth century about social, religious, and economic societies, including Aurora, concluded, "Keil was content to establish a community where a few dozen families might enjoy peace and moderate prosperity, while they kept alive in an alien environment the mellow culture of the German commoner."[2]

The stories of these few dozen families, enjoying peace and moderate prosperity, continue to be told.

The Families

Wilhelm and Louisa Keil

Wilhelm Keil was of great importance as the leader of the Aurora and Bethel colonies. In German, *Keil* means "wedge," and, indeed, Keil could be arbitrary. It's said that to those with whom he had a dispute he assigned housing some distance from the village. Once, he even engineered a market road into Aurora proper around land belonging to a farmer with whom he was arguing. One couple waited thirty years before marrying, as Keil would not consent. (They married after his death and after the dissolution of the colony because combined asset shares offered to single men and women were larger than those offered to a married couple.)

However, people saw that Keil kept them safe and prosperous, and few families openly disagreed with him for long. Besides, Keil could be generous. He had a home built for Frederick and his young bride, Louisa Giesy, in much the pattern of his *Grosse Haus*. The Frederick Keil home still stands in private ownership not far from where the church was built on the top of the village's highest hill.

Male colonists were skilled craftsmen, creating function and beauty as displayed in this tin lantern, similar to what Christian Giesy, a tinsmith, might have made. Imagine how the design scattered sprays of light on cabin walls while keeping any wind at bay. (ACHS collection.) *JK photo*

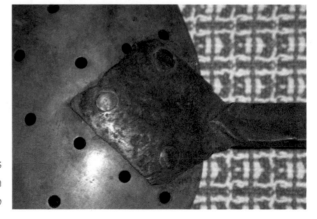

A brass ladle demonstrates the colonist craftsman's passion for making beautiful even the practical: a stylish arrow joins handle to bowl. (ACHS collection.) *NL photo*

Emma Wagner Giesy's Running Squares on Point quilt (also seen on the cover and in part 5) in front of the Aurora Colony's Emma Wakefield herb garden. *JK photo*

Oral tradition indicates that Keil's daughters and granddaughters quilted. Granddaughter Aurora Keil's pattern of Appliquéd Birds on Wool (page 28) is one of the few remaining artifacts of the Keil family. Using a buttonhole stitch, Aurora handquilted the sandwich and used blue ties to bind the flannel back. One can see a small mistake with white thread where she started over—perhaps the wool too thick for her small hands to quilt through the batting—and can imagine her mother redirecting her efforts.

The stylized bird became associated with the colony, appearing on the corner of another colorful quilt specifically made for the Keil family and on a handmade box with wire hinges and the name *W. F. Keil* inside. Tinsmiths made the bird design into a cookie cutter, and one imagines such sugar cookies appearing on the tables at the Aurora Hotel or traveling with a child on his family's train trip home to Portland.

A quilt of stunning colors of blue and red and gray called Tumbling Blocks (page xvi) was found in the Keil house, where a previous owner discovered it masquerading as stuffing for a couch. The thirteen hundred and sixty-five wool pieces include navy and black mourning cloth, deep red solids, and black stripes that would be worn by those grieving—all finely stitched and the colors expertly placed to give three-dimensional depth.

For many years, Wilhelm Keil was the only "doctor" for the colony, untrained formally in medicine but a skilled herbalist using homeopathic cures. The herb garden was a staple, divided into four areas representing its value and usefulness: cooking, medicine, tea, and fragrance.

Today, the garden sending forth fragrance in the Aurora museum courtyard brandishes similar herbs planted in the Old Economy Village garden in Pennsylvania. Dedicated by the Aurora Colony Museum Board in 1974,

Emma Wagner Giesy, a skilled quilter and the only female scout sent west. *ACHS photo*

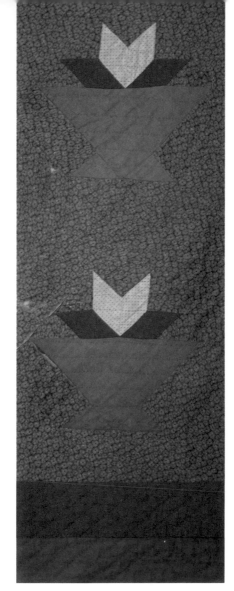

Ida Giesy Becke's Basket Variation quilt. (Circa 1875–1900; 84.75 x 86.25 inches; ACHS collection.) *NL photo*

it was named for Emma Wakefield, a native of Maine who spent thirty-four years in the town of Canby, neighboring Aurora, as a nationally recognized herbalist. Emma grew herbs in her home, assisted in the garden's creation, spoke often to groups, and shared her knowledge of herbs with the Oregon Museum of Science and Industry.[3]

Dr. Keil modeled such sharing. He offered healing services to people in the surrounding community with the conviction to help those in need, whether members of the colony or not. So in late 1862, when colonist John Wolfer sought permission from Dr. Keil to assist a neighbor suffering from smallpox, Keil said yes. Weeks later, four of Keil's own children—Elias (nineteen), Louisa (eighteen), Gloriunda (fifteen), and Aurora (thirteen)—succumbed to smallpox. A fourth daughter, Amelia, survived, though she also died a few years before either Keil or his wife. Sons Frederick, Emanuel, and August (the latter also an herbalist, though said to be less skilled than his father) survived their parents.

Quilts must have brought comfort to the Keil family that winter of 1862–63. One can imagine Louisa Keil, remembering young Aurora and her older sisters before their deaths, agreeing with the colonist who wrote, "Mama and I are quilting. Wish you were here so you could help us."[4] Perhaps when geese flew south across the village or birds chattered in the treetops, the memory of stitching warmth brought comfort to the surviving Keils.

Ida Giesy Becke, daughter of Emma and her second husband, Jack Giesy, was a fine colony quilter who married a carpenter. *ACHS photo*

The Giesy and Wagner Families and Descendants

Emma Wagner Giesy chose blue, teal, and red, colony favorites, for many of her quilts. These were bold choices made by dyeing hand-spun threads. Such intense colors in a woolen quilt were fitting for the colony's only woman scout, who crossed the continent on horseback from Bethel, Missouri, to the Northwest—while pregnant. Her daughter, Ida Giesy Becke, when she was old enough, later selected those colors along with purple, the color of sunrise against the glaciers of Mount Hood.

In 1853, Emma gave birth to her first son, Andrew, in Steila-

Martin Giesy's pharmacy and medical cabinet. Professionally trained, Martin served as the colony's physician for many years. He was brother to Christian Giesy and uncle to Emma and Christian's children, the older of whom he apprenticed at a young age. (ACHS collection.) *NL photo*

coom, Washington Territory, at the military fort there. With her husband, Christian Giesy, and the other scouts sent from Bethel, she helped carve out life in the wilderness. Challenges included building in the coastal forest and having their efforts rejected by Wilhelm Keil when he arrived with his deceased son and the first wave of Bethel immigrants.

This Nine Patch on Point quilt, handpieced and handquilted by Emily Giesy Miller, 1879–90, has one Monkey Wrench block at the center. Was Emily making a statement or stirring something in the colony? Her arrangement of colors demonstrates showmanship. The quilt, a two-inch-square grid, is made of wool and commercially manufactured fabric, with the setting blocks in colony manufactured homespun blue and red, while the top features pieced blue and red plaid, bordered with madder sides. The border is a homespun red. (60.5 x 76.5 inches; ACHS collection.) *JK photo*

A niece of Emma Wagner Giesy, Emily Giesy Miller, is the maker of the Nine Patch on Point quilt with one Monkey Wrench block (left). The blocks at right are from the Nine Patch on Point bed quilt made by Catherine Miley Steinbach. It's likely that she and her mother worked on this quilt together, piecing the cotton scraps of polka dot, small floral, and plaid. Both hand- and machine-pieced, the quilt includes a center block of indigo. (Circa 1880–1910; 78 x 78.5 inches; ACHS collection.) *JK photo*

The Giesy (Gisy) family that Emma married into was of Swiss origin and prominent in the colony's history. Andreas and Barbara (née Giesy) had fourteen children, of whom Christian was the oldest. The Giesys first encountered Wilhelm Keil in Pennsylvania and continued to follow him into Missouri, as had Emma Wagner Giesy's family. Several of the Giesys—John, Andrew, Helena, Christian, and Martin—held prominent places within the colony organization.

Christian Giesy worked as a tinsmith for the colony. A trusted servant, he recruited many long-term members into the Bethel group, men who later followed him to Washington and Oregon. Each recruiter also had a trade, and Christian's pressed-tin lanterns and the tin spoons made by others show marked attention to detail. Often at the items' joints, the artisan added some small flair to give the piece hint of individuality. Such additions weren't necessary for proper function, but they suggest an understanding of the human spirit's need to be singular as well as purposeful, and for craft to be its voice.

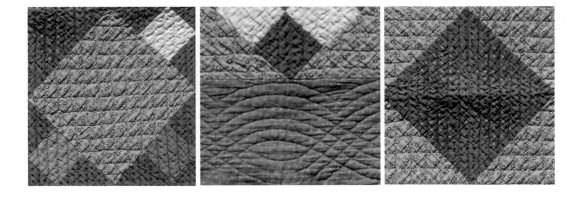

The Wagner family was influential in Keil's Bethel colony, but most did not arrive in Aurora until 1862. Back row, standing from left: Catherine, Louisa, Johanna. Front row, seated from left: David and Emma (who married Christian Giesy, not shown). Jonathan (not shown) was a clerk for the colony and built Emma's house for her. William (also not shown) lived in Phillipsburg at the time of the photo, arriving later in Oregon. *Private collection photo*

Christian drowned in Willapa Bay in 1857. Emma witnessed this event, and descendants say it marked the remainder of her life with grief and yet determination. On her Running Squares quilt, Emma Giesy stitched in double crosses the initials CG for her husband or son, both named Christian. Some suggest this might be a laundry mark, as the women did their wash communally, but only one other Aurora quilt bears such embroidered initials, and Emma's quilt would have been recognized as uniquely hers, for she was a revered seamstress. Worn spots show the quilt's usefulness and may have been begun before she even headed west, the only woman in the scouting party. After Christian's death, and despite her desperate move from Willapa to Aurora in 1861, the quilt remained with her, a treasure.

Carpenter's Wheel with Star Center was handpieced and handquilted by Triphena Forstner Will, Aurora's premier colony quilter. Triphena was married to a carpenter. (Circa 1890–1910; 92 x 91 inches; private collection.) *NL photo*

Detail of Carpenter's Wheel with Star Center

Emma remained in the Willapa country for several years after her husband's death. Perhaps she wished to cling to the good memories of what the couple had begun there, to prove Dr. Keil wrong for leaving and going 120 miles south to Aurora. She was pregnant at Christian's death and had two small children to care for, and census records show she remained in her own home even though her in-laws lived a few miles away.

In 1860, she married a second time to a relative of Christian's, Jacob Giesy. It was not a good decision, so upon the birth of her fourth child, a girl, Ida, Emma fled with her children to a place of refuge: Aurora.

The house still stands that was built for her there when her name came up on the colony list; her home uniquely had two front doors (one an entrance to the kitchen/social area, and one an exit from the parlor). In later years, her seamstress skills were recognized and she was given the colony sewing machine for use in her home. Her parents and brothers and sisters later joined her, and all re-

Henry Ehlen brought this violin across the Oregon Trail and through the years kept the silk textile to wrap it. A carpenter and musician, Henry was known for both his reed- and basket-making skills. (Private collection.) *JK photo*

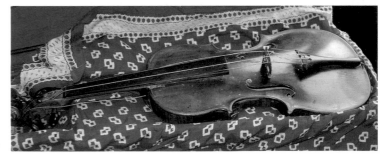

mained in the area. Colony records note that, strangely enough, Emma didn't officially join the colony until 1874, thirteen years after she arrived in Aurora.

Andrew Giesy Jr., brother to Christian, was a trustee of activities back in Bethel. A tanner by trade, he was well respected in the communal society, and it's likely Keil missed his wise counsel. Later correspondence suggests strain in the relationship, as Keil sent his own son back to assist in managing Bethel's affairs. Andrew arrived later in Aurora, after the deaths of Keil's children, and continued to serve the colony well. He became Keil's financial advisor and later the executor of his estate. His daughter, Emily, was a prolific quilter. Many of her quilts remain in the colony's collection.

John Giesy, Christian and Andrew's brother, came with his wife, Barbara, arriving in Willapa, Washington Territory, by ship in the winter of 1855. Though John had been a trusted follower of Keil, he remained with his father and siblings in the Willapa country, serving as the school superintendent. In October 1860, his father died, and in 1861, he brought south his widowed mother and eight children, including his oldest daughter, Elizabeth, a fine quilter, and his youngest sister, Louisa.

Catie Giesy, the daughter of Emma and Christian, stitched this sampler. Many samplers were punch kits with designs stenciled onto paper that was punched through in stitching. (15 x 15.5 inches framed; ACHS collection.) *JK photo taken in a house built for colonist Frederick Keil, still featuring its original wood floors and brick work from the 1860s*

Sampler by Johanna Wagner (pictured on page 40). Note the similarity in the urn with the sampler on the left, which was completed by Johanna's niece. (Circa 1840s; 24 x 25.5 inches framed; private collection.) *JK photo*

The Giesy women colonists, dressed in tailored finery. Customers from surrounding communities relied on Aurora's tailoring skills, contributing to the colony's economic success. *ACHS photo*

The oldest colony barn still standing is at the Giesy site, now owned by descendants. The window in the old barn is believed to be the bottom half of a window from the colony's church, one with a Gothic arch (see dedication page), rescued by the Giesys or Wills when the church was torn down in 1911. John built a large, three-story colony home designed not with a center staircase but rather with the stairs at one end. The house rose across a ravine from *Das Grosse Haus* and is lived in today by descendants of the Will family.

Helena, the oldest Giesy daughter, was beloved by many, according to descendants. She remained single, devoted her time to helping at the school, and was a faithful supporter of Dr. Keil. Census information shows she lived with the Keil family in *Das Grosse Haus*. She played a mandolin, known as a cittern, distinguished by a carved bear head on the neck, which is in the colony collection.

Louisa, the youngest Giesy girl, married into the Keil family by joining with Frederick. The couple lived just down the hill from the Keils, and this home still stands, surrounded by hickory trees whose starts were brought from Bethel.

Martin Giesy became first a pharmacist and then a physician for the colony. He remained in Willapa until 1861, then came to Aurora. Emma and Christian Giesy's son, Andrew, apprenticed with Martin in the pharmacy, and colony documents show that he and Christian, Emma's younger son, lived with Martin in Aurora from the time Andrew was eight years old until adulthood. This arrangement is without official explanation, though it was a practice in some families of the time that sons be raised by uncles if the father died.

Emily Giesy, Emma Giesy's niece, became an exceptional quilter, stitching patterns with names like Monkey Wrench and Bay Leaf. A Crazy quilt demonstrates this young woman's artistry in the use of simple shapes and color and suggests that fiber arts continued to give voice to the artistic nature of these colonists. A replica of the Bay Leaf quilt pattern is included at the end of this book.

Using rose-colored wool thread on a black background, Emily stitched a sampler dated 1876. She included the words *To Father* and MOTHER and *From EMILY,* which suggest that the sampler was more a gift to her mother than her father, but that Father could not be ignored.

The Giesys were considered confidants of Keil, both encouragers and wise. The men offered official advice as colony trustees; the women likely made suggestions to their husbands over meals or while putting warming pans under the covers as couples prepared for bed. Each had her way of influencing, though women's voices were not so easily heard.

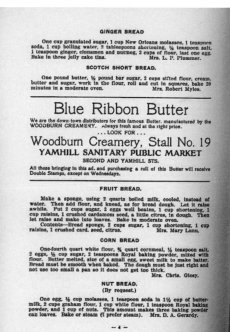

Excerpts from the 1915 Kenilworth Presbyterian Cookbook. Catherine Ehlen, Emma Giesy's daughter, was partial to spinach and apparently not concerned about cholesterol. (Private collection.) *JK photo*

Elizabeth Giesy Kraus handpieced the all-cotton Broken Dishes quilt top, circa 1875–1900, 75 x 75 inches, with plaids, calicos, geometric stripes, and paisleys that suggest shattered plates. Aurora Colony quilters in the twentieth century finished the quilting. Colony men turned the spool bed frame and made the trunk. The textile carpet was handwoven on a wagon wheel form, diameter 34 inches. Over the footboard is Lost Ships by an unknown maker, circa 1870s, 72 x 78.5 inches. (ACHS collection.) *JK photo*

The Extended Giesy Family

Karl Ruge, a university-trained teacher and, later, keeper of the toll bridge at Aurora, traveled west with Keil, but he remained in Washington when Keil vacated to Oregon. Christian Giesy had recruited the educator years before, and he served as the instructor both in Willapa and later in Aurora. Once Professor Wolff arrived, he and Ruge became responsible for educating both boys and girls in Aurora, along with the help of music director Henry C. Finck.

The 1860 census in Willapa shows Karl living with Sebastian Giesy and his wife, who had also taken in a Giesy cousin, Jacob. The communal household lived next door to the widowed Emma and her three children, with Jacob eventually becoming Emma's second husband.

Emma Giesy's daughter from her second marriage, Ida, left a legacy through her quilts, and it's believed that she and her mother worked on several together. Ida's Basket Variation (page 36) was donated to the Aurora Colony Historical Society by her granddaughter in 1984; the gift prevented the quilt from being lost to the winds of Hurricane Katrina in 2005.

Elizabeth Giesy Kraus

Ida married Henry Becke, a respected carpenter in the colony. Colonists built lathes and turned spool tables and beds. Like other colony women, Ida must have stretched quilt covers over a frame raised above the bed when hands weren't stitching them. Carpenters were called upon for the fine-tooled work that adorned some of the later colony homes: detailing interior molding, building pie cabinets and coolers, and forming everything from looms to stools. Quilts such as Carpenter's Wheel bear witness to their influence and skill.

Catherine Giesy Ehlen, Emma's older daughter, was born in the Willapa country. Though no quilts by her are known or remain, a sampler with her signature is in the museum collection. She may have developed an interest in music since her husband's family made reeds and one carried a violin across the 1863 trail; she was known for her culinary interests.

Despite her difficult second marriage, Emma obviously supported marriage, as all four of her children married. In later years, Emma lived with Catherine and her family in Portland, Oregon. Both women attended the Kenilworth Presbyterian Church, just a few doors down from the Ehlen home, and offered recipes in the 1915 cookbook published by the church's Ladies Aid Society. A favorite recipe of Emma's was Strawberry Cake: "One-half cup butter, 2 eggs, 1 1/2 cups flour, 1 cup stewed strawberries, 1 teaspoon soda dissolved in the juice of these berries. Bake in layers or loaf."[5] No suggestions were given for heat or how long to bake, issues dependent upon humidity and a woman's oven. Perhaps the recipe reminded Emma how colonists would pick strawberries and hold an annual festival for the fruit that grew wild in the part of Oregon affectionately called Eden.

Catherine Ehlen might have made her mother's doughnuts or corn bread, other recipes provided by "Mrs. Chris Giesy" in that 1915 cookbook; she was partial to German Spinach and apparently not concerned about cholesterol.

Emma wrote to her parents in 1861 urging them to join her in Aurora. David and Catherina Wagner, with Emma's sisters and brothers, eventually arrived in Aurora, traveling from Bethel in 1862. They operated a mill and later purchased property along the Willamette River to raise turkeys. David Wagner Sr. and Andreas Giesy had been early followers of Wilhelm Keil, who had asked them to help manage affairs at Bethel as he left for the Northwest. When the Wagners followed, the girls—Johanna, Louisa,

A china-head doll rests on an all-cotton Four Square reversible doll quilt, 12.5 x 18.5 inches, handpieced by an unknown maker. The miniature doll bed, with spindle-turned spool head- and footboards was made by colonists. On long winter nights colony men made toys (right) for their children and nurtured their youngsters' budding craft skills as well. (ACHS collection.)
JK photos

and Catherine—brought with them samplers and needlework with themes of houses, flowers, and stylized letters of the alphabet. It's believed that most surviving colony needlework was completed back in Bethel and brought with them, unframed, rolled up like socks, adding little weight on the journey. Several of the Wagner and Giesy descendants remain present-day physicians in the West.

In Aurora, Jonathan Wagner remained loyal to Keil, living in the colony and working in the store. He built a house for Emma at Keil's direction. The house, without the typical center hallway, had two front doors forming a U-shaped floor pattern and was later lived in by the George Kraus family. Descendants donated the house to the museum in 1969, which is why it's known as the Kraus House.

Like many Bethelites, the Wagners brought with them trunks painted red and blue—and all their children (Emma's siblings), including a foster daughter named Christine. Fostering and adopting children was a

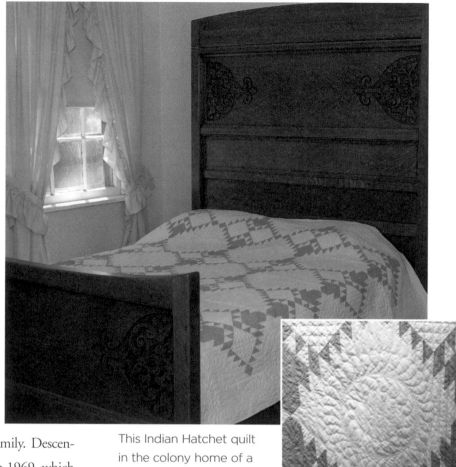

This Indian Hatchet quilt in the colony home of a descendant shows Triphena Forstner Will's exceptional quilting skill. The chambray blue and white cotton quilt is one of her finest. The backing is unbleached muslin with a thin cotton batting. (Circa 1880–1910; 72 x 78 inches; private collection.) *JK photo*. Lead pencil quilt marks are still visible on the detail, right. *JC photo*

Triphena may have dressed plainly, as other colony women did, but her artistic quilts remain magnificent and distinctive. *ACHS photo*

common practice among the followers of George Rapp, especially after that leader moved toward a policy of celibacy. Many Aurora descendants claim foster ancestors.

Of all the Wagner children, only Emma and her youngest brother, William, ever married. Her sisters and other brothers lived close to the colony though not always as a part of it. In 1874, Jonathan Wagner enabled his family to purchase property along the Willamette River with "gold coin" from the widow of Oregon's first territorial governor, George L. Curry.

In one of the last large migrations from Bethel to Aurora, a relative of Ida Giesy Becke's, Sarah Becke, arrived in 1867 with ten siblings. Charles Becke, Sarah's father, had been the shoemaker for the colony back in Nineveh, Missouri, one of the colony's offshoot communities. Sarah pieced the red and blue, hand-dyed cotton quilt called Ocean Waves. Accented with triangles in black and shades of green, the quilt gives the sense of the movement she may have experienced as she rode across the prairie. Her brother later took parts of the old wagon to craft a miniature wagon replica and wrote the story of the crossing on its canvas.

With several miniatures in the colony collection—dollhouses, wagons, and looms—one wonders if, as winter rains carpeted the Willamette Valley in green, men found respite in making small replicas to give their sons and daughters as Christmas gifts or a way to teach fine crafting skills. Or maybe their efforts connected them to days when their ancestors carved children's toys, such as tops, and intricate carousels turned by candles' heat. In Germany and the eastern states, such miniatures had

---

And all that believed were together, and had all things common; and sold their possessions and goods, and parted them to all men, as every man had need.

—ACTS 2:44–45, ABS

been crafted long before the 1800s and were often viewed as works of art worthy of emulation. In Aurora, long winters and abundant sources of wood made carving a natural craft.

Christian and Emma Giesy's sons might have played with such treasures, as they were active in the colony. Andrew served first as an apprentice to Martin Giesy in his pharmacy and, like his uncle, studied to be a physician. The colony sent Andrew to Willamette University and later to Pennsylvania for a specialty; he served the colony many years before opening a private practice in Portland, then serving as assistant superintendent of the Oregon State Hospital in nearby Salem. Christian Giesy became a farmer and carpenter and worked with his father-in-law, Henry Ehlen. Christian and his sister Catherine married a sister and brother from the Ehlen family, intertwining those family stories.

Colonist Benjamin Forstner, a cousin of Triphena, served as a colony gunsmith and designer of the patented Forstner bit, for which he won a prize at the 1876 Centennial Exposition in Philadelphia. Used widely by fine craftsmen today, the Forstner bit makes clean lines into wood. (ACHS collection.)
JK photos

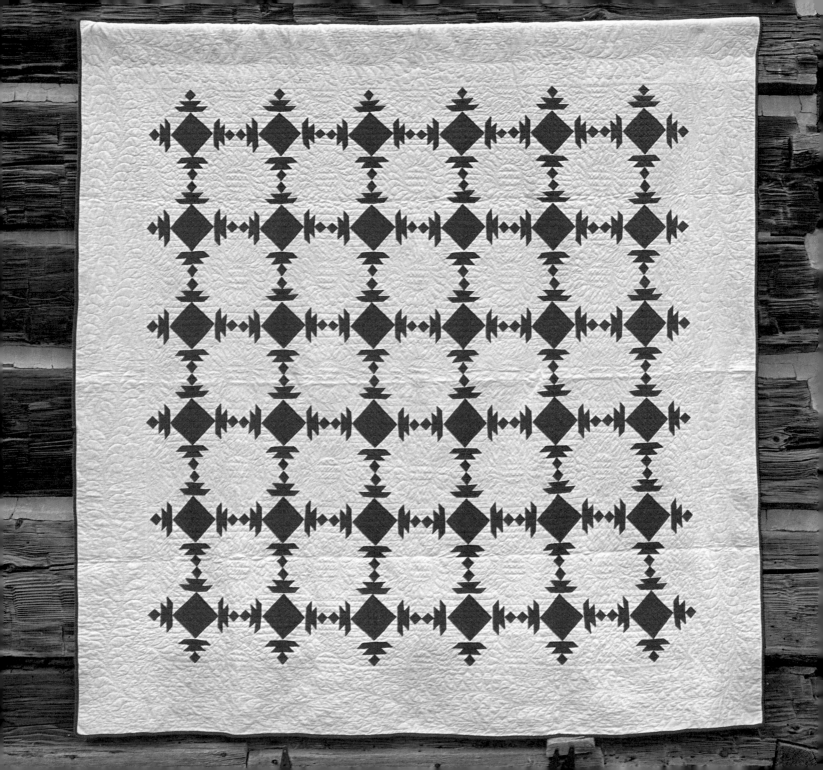

The Forstner-Will Families

Triphena Forstner Will, 1833–1927, was probably the most prolific quilt maker in the Aurora Colony. She arrived with her husband, Leonard, and their six-month-old son, Leonard Jr., in the 1863 wagon train along with 252 others. Benjamin Forstner, a cousin, arrived at the same time but remained in the colony only two years before departing for Salem, twenty-five miles southwest. Benjamin "became a gunsmith and also an inventor, patenting a new type of drill bit known as the 'Forstner bit,'"[6] still in use by craftsmen and carpenters for the crisp circular cut it makes into wood.

Triphena's cousin Rosa married August Keil in 1864, intertwining yet another colony family with the Keils. The oldest surviving son of Wilhelm and Louisa Keil, August had been sent back to Bethel to act as his father's agent, and there he remained the rest of his life.

Another Forstner cousin, Elizabeth, became a well-known cook in the Aurora Hotel, while her sister Catherine married Henry Snyder. The Snyders had five children, all but one who left Aurora to join secular society— signs of the loosening grip that Keil had on the lives of those who remained behind in Bethel for ten years without his direct influence.

Triphena's surviving quilts, often loaned by descendants to the colony for exhibition, illustrate a high artistic understanding of pattern and design. Triphena lived to be nearly ninety years old, and her quilts have stood the test of time for their vibrancy and delicate detail. Her

Pine Burr quilt, handpieced by Triphena Forstner Will, photographed against the caulked logs of the 1865 Stauffer-Will farmhouse. It's made of all cotton, and the quilting is ten stitches per inch. Setting (or plain) blocks feature a quilted feather wreath with a colony crosshatch center. The border is quilted as a feathered plume with a unique flowering vine on both sides, twelve stitches per inch, with some quilting marks still faintly visible on the detail, right. (Circa 1880; 80 x 78.5 inches; private collection.) *JK photos*

Barn and outbuildings of the 1865 Stauffer-Will farmstead on a blustery spring day.
Note the hops field at right in the background. *NL photo*

Indian Hatchet is a crosshatch quilt showing a feather wreath. Handstitched, it shows a double row of stitching considered among the finest of colonist quilting skill. Whig's Defeat Variation is an astounding quilt, with colors rich and vibrant to this day, reflecting the tender care given by descendants. Seeing these quilts, one can almost hear women's chatter reaching to the oak rafters of a colony home as they quilted a Double Irish Chain with its vibrant blues. Union Square, another detailed utility quilt, would have consumed hours of time between tending family and putting up preserves to line the cool root-cellar shelves.

Two quilts airing on the porch of the Stauffer-Will farmhouse. Catherine Steinbach made the Multichain Variation quilt (at left), circa 1880, 75 x 75.5 inches, handpiecing a treasured sampling of printed cottons from the period and handquilting thirteen stitches per inch. The maker of Log Cabin (at right), circa 1880–1910, 67 x 74 inches, is unknown. The calico backing was handtied through cotton batting, using red yarn. The detail shows Catherine's Multichain Variation. Dozens of two-inch squares were quilted through both diagonals. Setting blocks feature crossed feathers with crosshatching in the triangle; the border is quilted in a cable pattern. (ACHS collection.) *JK photos*

The Stauffer Family

John Stauffer, one of the original 1853 scouts, remained for a time in Willapa with Christian and Emma Giesy and all of Christian's family once they arrived from Bethel. Several other scouts remained as well.

John Stauffer went to Aurora in 1865 and for the next year built his farmhouse, a two-story log home with an attic, now a showcase of the Old Aurora Colony Museum. The farmhouse's construction represents the finest in German building techniques, including a root cellar beneath the house, something common to colony homes but unique to other Oregon and Washington settlements. Basements and tornado shelters weren't needed in this mild-winter climate as they had been in Missouri and places farther east, but the cool storage kept hams, fruits,

Nine Patch utility quilt at the Stauffer-Will farmhouse, 72 x 74 inches, maker unknown, hand-pieced, mostly wool and cotton batting, diagonally handquilted. It might have been used during travel, in the barn, or as an extra covering for many overnight visitors. (ACHS collection.) *JK photos*

and vegetables nearly as fresh for later consumption as when first picked. Basements also allowed for sausage making; cool air eased grinding and stuffing work. In John Giesy's still-standing colony house, the sausage recipe is written on a wide ceiling beam, and everyone apparently knew what to do with the ingredients: "100 lbs. meat, 1³/₄ lb. salt, 4 oz. pepper."

The wedge-tail log construction, fine caulking, and shake roofing has kept the farmhouse in prime condition despite its age. Surrounded by a 135-year-old maple, an old barn, and a chicken and hog house, one can step back into the nineteenth century as easily as walking down a flight of wooden steps.

As a nine-year-old, Christina Wolfer (right, with her brother George and sister Sarah) witnessed another brother destroy all her mother's dishes on the Oregon Trail—except for one small butter plate. *ACHS photo.* How her mother, Catherine, must have wept over the loss of those dishes, and what presence of mind she had to save at least one. (ACHS collection.) *JK photo*

When Walls Talk

In the Stauffer-Will farmhouse, an unusual discovery appeared inside the wall between the kitchen and living room. Next to remnants of German newspapers used for wallpaper and insulation, Gail Robinson, a volunteer and Aurora Colony Historical Society board member, located bits of cloth meant to span the gaps between planks. She also found tiny scraps of wallpaper that bore resemblance to William Morris designs. Another attic search revealed several rolls of old wallpaper, including a larger roll of that tiny scrap from the downstairs wall.

Gail photographed a sample and sent it to Charles Rupert Designs, which makes period reproductions, hoping for help in identifying and dating. Searching for the length and width that the design company needed, volunteers located two more designs believed to date from around 1870–80.

Now the company is reproducing these designs for the colony to paper a room and will include information about the origin with every roll sold—yet one more way the colony's history and preservation is shared with the larger world.

ACHS collection. *NL photo*

The Steinbach Cabin, now maintained on the colony grounds, is used during the quilt show and for village educational programs for children and adults. (ACHS collection.) *JC photo*

Stauffer women would have sat on the back porch with hoop in hand, making the tiny double row of stitches for which many colony quilters are known.

John Stauffer's oldest son, Jacob, married Matilda Knight, sister of one of the original scouts. Matilda was a superb quilter, known especially for her blue and white Bear Paw and the spectacular Sunflower quilt composed of primary colors. Jacob's eight sisters could have worked on that quilt, as Matilda may have begun it before traveling from Bethel or while waiting out the winter in Willapa. Yet the perfectly spaced, double-chain stitches suggest only Matilda's handcrafting.

Matilda died in 1867 giving birth to twins, one of whom survived and was given her mother's name. Jacob's sisters raised the infant, likely making baby quilts like the pink and white Nine Patch made by Elizabeth Wolfer Zimmerman, now in the colony collection (see the replica pattern on page 136). Matilda's life quilt (the Sunflower, featured in part 2 of this book) was handed down to her daughter, who married August Will, and later descendants kept it as a precious reminder of life's fragility and the comfort of stitched goods.

Jacob's second wife, Christina Wolfer, carries the legacy of hardships on the trail from Bethel with a beautiful butter plate once believed lost. In 1926, colony descendant Clark Moor Will noticed this plate. He was visiting Ida Stauffer, who told how Catherine Wolfer, wife of Rudolph, had packed the family's prized china for the 1863 trip from Bethel, Missouri, to Aurora, Oregon. Their daughter Christina (later to marry Jacob) was just nine years old when she witnessed the wrath of her brother Samuel, who discovered this "useless truck" in the belongings. Samuel, having experienced great difficulties on the trek, flew into a rage at the excess weight of the china and began breaking each piece over rocks. His mother saved this one sample and hid it in cornmeal for the rest of the trip. How she must have grieved, prevented from intervening, helplessly watching her son smash those dishes. What presence of mind to have saved at least one piece.

Colonists could trade for necessary items at the colony stores in both Bethel and Aurora as in this 1875 account for the Steinbach store. In the early years of the colony, the only woman to have her own ledger page was Emma Giesy. Other women's purchases of calico and thread were recorded on a page for a father, husband, brother, or son. *ACHS photo*

Grace Miley, nearly upstaged by her dog in Shelbyville, Missouri, later came to Aurora. Colonists included their dogs in both studio and everyday photographs. *ACHS photo*

Christina's daughter, Ida, had possession of the plate until 1926, and it was eventually inherited by a descendant, but no one seemed to know where "Christina's Plate" had gone until 2007. That's when Nina McCoy brought her fifteen-year-old son, Andrew, to tour the Stauffer-Will farmstead, as she had only seen it from afar, once it left the family's hands. Andrew took notes and snapped pictures he planned to turn into a paper for a high-school class. At the conclusion of the tour, Nina was asked if she had any colony artifacts. "Well, there is this one plate," she told the curator. Nina donated the treasure to the museum, where the story is told again and again.

Christina Stauffer was also known as a highly creative quilt maker. She married William Wolfer, while another sister, Hannah, married Jacob Steinbach at her family's log home on September 3, 1876:

It was a festive occasion and a bright sunny morning when I ran half a mile across fields to be at a double wedding ceremony at the Stauffer log house—Music from a pick-up orchestra waxed clear and beautiful… a table ran the full length of the dining hall loaded with food.[7]

A pick-up orchestra included whoever happened to arrive with instruments in hand. One can imagine the scent of lavender pervading the festivities as sausage, sauerkraut, and strudels were swallowed to the tunes of minuets, waltzes, and some rousing German marches.

The Steinbach-Miley Families

Catherine Miley was the firstborn child of Frederick Jacob Miley and Mary Ann Link. (George Link, a relative, was one of the early scouts sent west). Mary Ann died in 1855 giving birth to twins in Missouri; Catherine, then only nineteen, assumed the responsibility of caring for her father, five brothers, and one sister. She married George Steinbach in 1861 in Nineveh, Missouri; they moved to Aurora in 1875 with their five children. By 1876 they made their home in the sturdy two-room log cabin with a loft standing on today's museum grounds. And it's Catherine who recounts how Dr. Keil, like so many fathers then, danced with her as an eight-year-old girl, her soles on the toes of his leather shoes.

The Steinbachs were well regarded in the colony. Adam Steinbach (later chosen as a trustee) was a signer

This Crazy quilt by an unknown maker may have been a studio prop, but Christina Stauffer Wolfer (second from left) was a fine quilter and it's unlikely she'd want any quilt but her own in a family photograph. *ACHS photo—the sole image showing colonists with a recognizable quilt*

in 1866 when the Aurora Colony composed the Articles of Agreement outlining expectations and freedoms granted to members as citizens of the greater United States. Upon Dr. Keil's death, Phillip Steinbach, an attorney, was one of five Bethelites sent to Aurora to help finalize the distribution of property.

While the men organized and made covenants, the women spun and stitched. Catherine was no exception. Many of her quilts, believed to have been worked on by both Catherine and her mother, were donated to the museum by descendants. Imagine the comfort they must have given Catherine in later years, knowing she'd worked with her mother to piece them together. She could hold the memory in her hands.

The Wolfer-Zimmerman Families

Elizabeth Wolfer Zimmerman is remembered in part for walking the entire Oregon Trail, carrying her infant daughter, Kate, all the way from Elim, Missouri, to Aurora in 1863. Women often walked beside the wagons rather than riding in them to save space and the mule team's strength. Kate was wrapped in a baby quilt Elizabeth had made herself.

Aunt Mary Zimmerman, a "spinster," and Margaret Stauffer, with whom Mary lived, handquilted this Crazy quilt. Constructed of mixed fabrics—corduroy, velvet, silk, wool, and cotton—the pieces are all shapes and sizes and overstitched with feather-stitch embroidery. Detail of the Crazy quilt shows a green ribbon stitched into the front block that reads *Willamette Trading Company, Barlow,* referencing a settlement near Aurora. The Huldamay Giesy family of Willapa, Washington, who tended this quilt, reports that after her family visits to Aurora in the early 1900s, they often returned with a quilt given as a gift by colony quilters, for which they were grateful. (Circa 1890-1910; 69.5 x 82.5 inches; ACHS collection.) *JK photos*

Colonist Henrietta Wolfer, known as Retta, never married and wasn't a quilter, instead preferring to read and play piano and cello. *ACHS photo*

Three years previous, in 1860, Elizabeth married David Zimmerman Jr. and made the wedding shirt he wore, now in the collection at the Aurora Colony Historical Society. His initials are embroidered in tiny stitches on the tail.

Besides making several quilts, the Zimmermans were fine letter writers, corresponding with relatives and friends back in Elim and Bethel and with aunts who lived a few miles down the road:

> I have so much sewing to do yet and I also want to knit two pair of stockings for Hulda yet before winter and made two shirts for Henry last week—also most of my small sewing is done but we need some new things— bed clothes and comforters etc.[8]

The Kraus Family

Elizabeth Giesy Kraus worked as a seamstress in the colony tailor shop. She married George Kraus and lived for nearly fifty years in the colony home known as the Kraus House. George was the colony shoemaker, and ledgers from the colony store contain drawings of members' feet for his use in making leather boots or slippers. Only one foot was needed per person since shoes were made as one-foot-fits-both.

The Kraus House is believed to have been built by Jonathan Wagner in 1863–64 for his sister Emma Giesy and her children, though they lived there but a few years. Elizabeth and George moved into this double-front-door colony home in 1880 after their wedding and remained there. Their son donated the house to the museum, along with most of its furnishings, in 1969; it was moved from its original site in the village to where it now stands beside the Oxbarn Museum. Several of the quilts in the colony collection were additional donations by the Kraus family.

Since 1969 the house has been the site of weaving and spinning demonstrations, and countless tours have told the stories of the colonists, bringing their history to life. A Nine Patch bedsack, an early sleeping bag, made by the Scholl-Wolfer family represents others likely used by additional guests when family members visited or perhaps stayed too late to drive their buggies home. Elizabeth also made the Cheater Star doll quilt, called thus because blocks were composed of printed material rather than pieced. One can imagine the Kraus family members stitching in the large upstairs bedroom or working on samplers while chatting with friends in the parlor beside the blue-painted mantel.

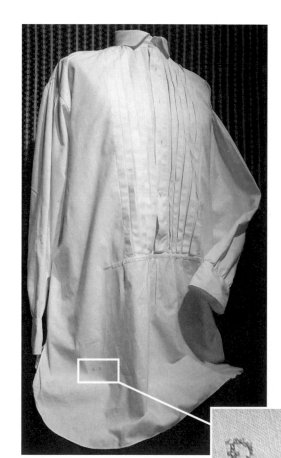

Elizabeth Wolfer Zimmerman made this cotton shirt for her husband, David, for their 1861 wedding. Note the stylized embroidered initials on the shirttail. Only three other colony textiles show any individualizing initials. (ACHS collection.) *JC photos*

Kraus family members on the porch of their home. This house with its unique two front doors—one to parlor and one to kitchen—was originally built for Emma Giesy, but the Kraus family lived in it much longer and donated it to the Aurora Colony Historical Society, which maintains it. *ACHS photo*

And the Others

There were many more families: Bauers and Gingers, Schaeffers and Snyders, Schueles and Frys.

It was the German practice for a son to be named for his father but given a different middle name; the son was then often called by that middle name. Girls, too, often bore their mothers' and grandmothers' names, so the historical records are dotted with Louisas, Catherines, Matildas, and Roberts, Michaels, and Henrys, all using the same last name—a reminder that the families were closely related and a complication in filling out family trees.

In the colony years, every Sunday afternoon, gathering at Park House might well have been considered a family reunion in Aurora. The bachelors and aunties, many who lived together, or the elderly living in family homes, found the gathering a way to catch up on news. The conversations would have been about crops, harvests, and trade for the men; and children, weddings, gardens, and clothing for the women. But all would have attended to the needs of others, for that was the colony way.

Stories are the sparks that light our ancestors' lives,
the embers we blow on to illuminate our own.

—JANE KIRKPATRICK

George Kraus, the colony shoemaker, with his grandson, approaching the Kraus House. The Leonard Will home is in the background. Generations lived in single family homes and supported one another. George made most of the colonists' shoes and also sold to surrounding areas. *ACHS photo*

Georgia Kraus, a quilter, snapping beans. In addition to textile arts, young girls were taught food preservation by their mothers and grandmothers. Families worked together, sharing virtues and stories. *ACHS photo*

Work

Called by a Daily Purpose

It must be remembered…that these people had
all their wants supplied and lived without care.…
Skilled artisans…could have gained vastly more
wealth if they had plied their trade in individualism.

—WILLIAM BEK, 1909

Few of us in this twenty-first century experience the works of our hands the way the men and women of Aurora did. We visualize vast projects requiring many minds and often years before we see completion. We stare at tiny screens for hours or work on fragments of a project. We frame a house but never participate in the finishing work of placing moldings around the doors or hanging cabinets in a kitchen. It's said that those entering the labor market in this twenty-first century will have as many as thirty different jobs over their working years. Even those who retire often begin a purposeful

Mary Schuele Rapps's Log Cabin / Barn Raising, circa 1850–75, 78 x 82 inches second career yet may not see a finished piece. We eat food we did not raise or preserve. At restaurants, we're served food we did not prepare. Housework is often denigrated, and some think of women's work as the brooms of society, brought out to clean houses and souls, then "put back in the corner until the next mess needs to be cleaned up."[1] We go to separate rooms or leave our homes to exercise, where our bodies engage in physical exertion with some temporal outcome—a thirty-minute workout. We achieve goals by engaging in competition with others, such as Ironman competitions, even though it's our personal best we seek. We walk to raise funds for treatment of diseases, finding community as we move along streets closed for temporary occasions.

Twenty-first-century work is rarely about creating a single product both functional and beautiful, and we often don't control the beginning, middle, or end of our labor. Consequently, we may never experience the sense of satisfaction and completion found in stitching a patchwork quilt used by a family member or friend, or working tin into patterns where candlelight casts delicate shadows against a hearth that warms our family with wood we chopped ourselves.

Our disconnection from work can often disconnect us from community.

In Aurora, everyone did their part. *ACHS photo*

Perhaps Mary Schuele's combination of light and dark material expressed her feelings about the thirty-year postponement of her marriage to Michael Rapps. After Dr. Keil's death, they waited four more years for the colony division of assets; as a married women, Mary would've received only half of what she did single.

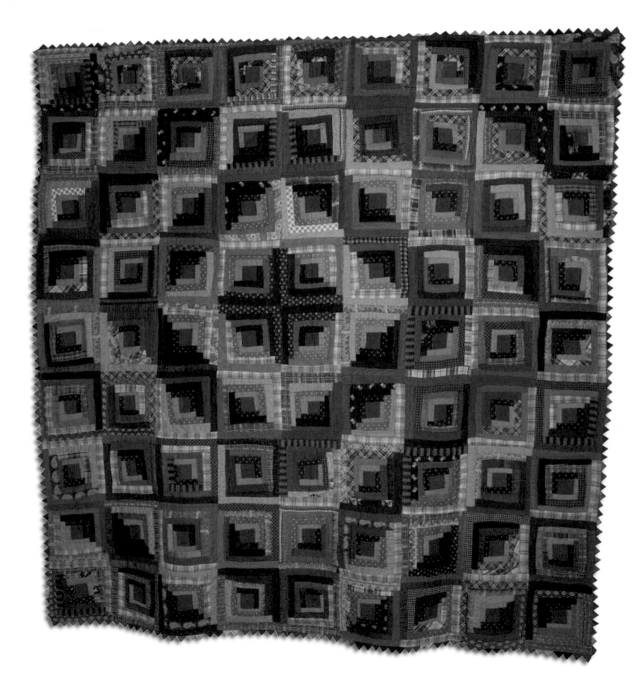

We don't know if Aurora colonists experienced angst within their work lives. Most would have believed they were created beings, born to create. Early artisans in the Old Testament, with which the colonists were familiar, are singled out for their creative bent, and many verses in Proverbs refer to virtues that would enhance the craftsman's role: discipline, humility, and diligence.[2] Craftsmen could see purpose in their daily labor, as Proverbs 22:29 offered: "Do you see a man skilled in his work? He will serve before kings; he will not serve before obscure men." The promise of legacy was wrapped into work.

"The craftsperson cannot ultimately be satisfied solely by making beautiful things, for he or she must find a place in the community,"[3] write contemporary theologians Robert Banks and R. Paul Stevens. This philosophy appears to be something the colonists understood. Made in their Creator's image, colonists co-created at many levels, beginning with family. The work of raising children may seem far removed from work, artistry, or craftsmanship, but there is mystery in both parenting and in living with uncertainty in the creative process. In *Let Your Life Speak,* Parker J. Palmer notes that if we are engaged in parenting, teaching, or healing, we find a meaningful life. Satisfaction is within the daily, mundane moments where we shape lives we're so invested in: our children's, grandchildren's, neighbor's, or a child who joins our table because his or her parents are still "at work."

Colonists and descendants raised their own sheep and harvested wool for their textiles. (ACHS collection.) *JK photo*

An array of yarn hand-dyed by colonists. (ACHS collection.) *JK photo*

Colonists kept separate households, and there was still the sense of extended family. They knew their neighbors' children and could keep a safe eye on them; children worked beside their parents, caring for elders, who in turn shared the secrets of canning beans or how to fix a broken wheel.

Work offered satisfaction; what one did had meaning for the entire community. The obligation of producing necessary things, with time to make them beautiful and individual, must have been fulfilling. A special occasion, such as a wedding, might have warranted finishing a quilt on time, but many textile projects were "life" projects bringing comfort in the effort, sharing hours with others, talking, and progressing without rush. A complicated

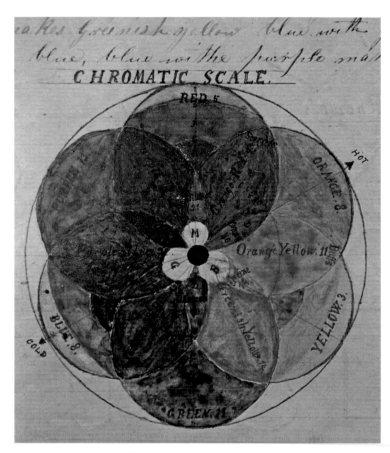

George Wolfer's chromatic scale found in his 1869 schoolbook with his notes on color mixing. (ACHS collection.) *PH photo*

pattern could be attempted, for there would be many hands and words of advice to see one through; satisfaction lived in process, not just completion. Letters between women often include a wish that the other was still near to work together and share stories.

Individuals Within Community

One mark of a communal society is the tension between the individual's needs and the group's. The Aurora colonists appear to have found a way to honor both through their artistry and craft. While communal, they still recognized individuality and often initialed their handwoven grain sacks or signed their creations with labels, not unlike craftsmen of old.

For a woman, the choice of quilt stitch used or whether to make a quilt reversible or not often served as a distinguishing feature. Colony quilt curator Annette James looks lovingly at colony textiles, identifying in the pieces chosen the qualities of a woman's personality and economic status. "She used old shirt fabrics to piece this block. Here, mourning cloth and different blues create the effect she wanted." Sometimes tiny dark spots on old fabrics can be recognized as bits of cotton seeds pushing through the bat, demonstrating its thinness or that it was cotton instead of wool. "Imagine her joy when she could afford to purchase enough material of one color to do the entire border and sash and didn't have to piece from worn clothing. She could create something totally new."[4] The size of Triphena Forstner Will's stitches, as tiny as a pinhead and double stitched, is a part of her signature.

Several colony women double stitched, creating two mirrored rows of stitches—ten to fifteen stitches per inch—to quilt the pieced cover to the backing.

Color served another way the colonists individualized their work and demonstrated joy and spiritedness in their everyday lives. In fact, by shades of color, Aurora Colony Historical Society curator Patrick J. Harris and others can identify a chest of drawers or bench as being colony produced. Harris recalls initial surprise at the variety of hues painted on colony buildings and furniture. He soon learned colonists manufactured their vivid dyes from natural sources for quilts, coverlets, and textiles. "This all made for a community of like-minded Christians living share and share alike in a village alive with color."[5]

A pie cupboard, painted in typical Aurora blue, holding colony-made kitchen tools. Note the square wooden butter forms on the first and third shelves, the handmade burled water dipper on the second shelf, and the Buena Vista pottery. Colonists traded their butter or crafts for stone pots thrown by Simon Way, a neighbor, and other local potters. Stoneware kept beans, salt pork, and other foods safe from marauding mice. (ACHS collection.) *JK photo*

Handmade wheelbarrow, painted Aurora blue, in the Stauffer-Will farmhouse root cellar. Women canned together, often in summer kitchens. Canning months were hot and steamy; the woodstove fires added to the discomfort. It's said the colonists sang as they worked...but one wonders. Perhaps they sang after the job was done, waiting for the lids to pop, indicating a good seal. (ACHS collection.) *JK photo*

Those who remember black-and-white television of the early 1960s might wonder how the shades of gray affected our views of early American life in the nineteenth century. Perhaps we saw that era as dark and dreary, with only enough energy to work, finding little time for play. Seeing Aurora's blue traveling trunks, bright green wagons with yellow trim, red-trimmed petticoats, and flashy color combinations using purple and red in quilts, make the colonists' lives more vivid—and more like our own.

One paint color common to the colony is known as Aurora blue—a prussian blue pigment mixed with white lead in an oil base. Colony store ledgers show this pigment purchased as early as 1857 and by the 1870s available commercially. Finished furniture showed variations on this shade, the variety caused by exposing a painted piece to light before adding another layer of paint. The longer each blue was exposed to the sun, the less a new blue darkened.

In 2007, David G. Wagner, MD, a colony descendant, removed chairs from his attic to take to a refinisher. Then he learned through a colony newsletter of chairs traditionally being painted blue. He immediately rescued his chairs and kept their original blue for posterity.

While wooden tools appeared to be left natural, other paint colors, like red and green, have been found on trunks, cabinets, pie safes, and other furniture. The varieties of color are obvious in the textiles, where natural dyes produced shades of red, blue, yellow, and green fabric. As Keil allowed land titles to be placed in individual names beginning in 1872, mostly to satisfy the younger generation, a wider range of colors and styles is noted, expressing even more individuality. Chair rails were painted bright blue with the wainscot below in another color such as pale pink, or even papered. Dark green or blue shades covered moldings. Fir floorboards were awash with the hues of sunrise and sunset, then splashed with bright rainbow-colored round rugs.

In the latter part of the colony period, both men and women had colorful calling cards (presented when visiting friends and neighbors) printed with floral designs.

Inside young George Wolfer's 1869 schoolbook, archivists found a chromatic scale, suggesting that tint and pigment were brought into even the most primary tollbooth-turned-schoolroom run by Professor Karl Ruge. It's likely colonists were surrounded by color, from

Typical Aurora kitchen featuring its chair of blue with rawhide seats. The circle rug, diameter 34 inches, was made of cotton and wool scraps and likely woven on a wagon wheel form to achieve the spoke pattern. (ACHS collection.) *JK photo*

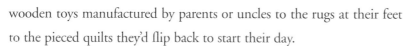

Colony calling cards. (ACHS collection.) *PH photo.* Below, round wool chair pillow, diameter 16 inches, hand-dyed by colonists. Handcrafted sewing box atop a colony cider box. The crafted stubble duck decoy awaits the fall hunting season in the wheat stubble field. (ACHS collection.) *JK photo*

wooden toys manufactured by parents or uncles to the rugs at their feet to the pieced quilts they'd flip back to start their day.

The use of color was complemented by an appreciation for pattern, and curator Patrick Harris believes colony designs may have anticipated artistic movements: "Colony quilts feature geometrical patterns that clearly foreshadow the abstract forms so common in the twentieth century."

Raw materials for the colonists' work came mostly from the land itself, and they made labor-saving devices, such as fruit dryers, apple presses, and looms of various sizes. They raised the plants for natural dyes; leather came from their cattle; wool came from their sheep. They raised flax and wove plaids and other wool patterns at their mill; while Aurora was never known as "the Belfast of Oregon," one Oregon editor in an early newspaper remarked it could be—the colony did exist in the heart of what became an important textile economy.

Nineteenth-century woolen mills in nearby Salem and the Jacob Brothers woolen mill founded in 1865 in nearby Oregon City employed many early settlers. Today commercial firms producing textiles of high quality, such as Pendleton Woolen Mills, still thrive on Northwest roots.

Families worked together to make such products a success, and the comfort afforded by a communal lifestyle allowed them to manufacture functional linens and other textiles that also featured detail and style. Design elements assigned to the simplest of their furniture pieces suggest that colonists appreciated beauty for beauty's sake. For example, the wardrobes colonists made featured graceful wooden hangers and pegs hung on movable racks similar to the tie racks found in walk-in closets today. Their washtubs, made by coopers, were painted vibrant colors. A courting bench, reminiscent of Amish ways by keeping young lovers sitting stiff and straight with plenty of space between them, was three-sided with the back and ends composed of turned spools much

Open-weave baskets, commonly handmade in Aurora, allowed moisture and water to run off while letting air circulate within. Picnic baskets also sported woven covers. A rim could be single wrapped with splints or double wrapped ("x-binding") for additional strength. This basket, probably brought from Bethel, shows the x-binding. Men made most of the baskets in the winter months. (Circa 1850s; ACHS collection.) *NL photo*

George Wolfer collected guns, many of which he sold to antiquarian Frederick Skiff in 1922 for one dollar each. Two guns on exhibit were loaned from grandchildren. George was a brickmaker and farmer, and ran a mineral spring. *ACHS photo*

like stacks of gracefully formed wooden bulbs handturned on lathes. If a union was successful, upon marriage the bench was turned toward the wall, making a perfect crib, with the wall serving as the fourth side.

Gunsmiths were as active in Aurora as they had been back in Bethel, bringing skills from European guilds. Men would have carved their own powder horns, made their own leather holsters, necessary for hunting game to supplement family and hotel meals, and carved duck decoys for the fall and winter bird migrations that peppered the skies above the Pudding River.

Above, colonists threshed wheat with horses, this one named Babe, with his owner simply Bill. Left, J. D. Hurst and Son owned the Aurora Roller Mills built after the colony dissolved. Colonists ran a grist mill for grinding their own and neighbor's wheat and operated a textile mill; the roller mill was a technological advancement. *ACHS photos*

In the fields, they grew potatoes, grain, and corn, and planted orchards that resulted in pear butter sold commercially and served at the Aurora Hotel. (Descendants still describe the pear butter as ambrosia to the tongue.) They sold a colony brew in the pub on the first floor of the hotel and crafted fine tools for everyday use: tin spoons, rope-bed tighteners, and oak-webbed baskets, each with a special forked branch for hanging, allowing both hands to be used for berry picking. Even fixing a wagon wheel took skill—reshaping at the blacksmith's forge with many hands to fit a tire around the wooden rim.

The colonists created objects that would wear well and fit comfortably in their hands; they were aware of such skill and that their products were desired in nearby villages. Woodworkers treaded the colony lathe to make the famous spool patterns found on their furniture. Blacksmiths and tinsmiths crafted buckets and lanterns but added special touches of design—the stylized bird, an extra flourish on a ladle joint, the double-wreath hand-stitched quilting pattern—distinctive to Aurora.

Many baskets that colonists used are believed to have been created in Bethel and brought west. With a loose weave of primarily ash and oak, the baskets were constructed with raised bottoms to allow water and air to flow through. Sides had strengthened weaves, and rims were made with single or double rows and crossed with Xs, also unique to Aurora. Oral tradition says men did most of the basket making: farmers during rainy winter months while the land lay fallow. The Ehlen family especially, according to oral tradition, made baskets in Aurora and fine music reeds as well.

Though it appears to be a candle snuffer, this slender object is a tin dinner horn, twelve inches long, made by colonists to call workers in from the fields. (ACHS collection.) *NL photo*

Everyone helped with threshing, including women. *ACHS photos*

Work Woven into the Colony Agreements

Each colonist appears to have understood that work was woven into community. The Articles of Agreement signed in 1866 noted in Article One the reason why each must work: so "all persons, with or without families…shall receive free lodging, board, clothing and washing and in case of sickness free medical attendance, medicines and nursing." Article Five expressed the value of compassion even beyond the colony: "That all sick, disabled or indigent persons, *outside the community,* who ask and merit our assistance, shall be relieved, as far as the means of our community can afford it." Article Eight reminded the colonists that each "must faithfully perform the daily labor assigned to him by the trustees or foremen of the community according to his trade or ability, and if a work of common interest is to be done, whereby more as (than) the usual hands are necessary, then

Aurora Colony Band members posing before one of their many performances. The band both entertained and served the colony's economy, as it charged for many performances and was in high demand. *ACHS photo, 1905*

every member or shopman is bound to follow the call for temporary help." There was even admonishment to "take good care of the tools and implements…[to] not suffer or allow that any of them should be injured or wasted."[6]

Descendants tell how women, too, worked side by side with men at harvest time, a task most likely added to daily meal preparation, child rearing, and household maintenance. Numerous photographs show men and women (and their dogs!) working together in the fields, but almost no photographs show the work we know women did at home or gathering in quilting groups.

While independent settlers in the region worked land claims on their own, the colonists worked together to support a common community. They took pleasure not in meeting the government's requirements to plant, build a house, and remain for five years, but to contribute so fellow colonists and outside neighbors would have food and shelter. Crafting uniqueness into work brought a meaningful dimension to everyday life.

"I am working at my old trade," wrote the blacksmith Joseph Burkholder in a letter dated June 27, 1864, to friends back in Bethel. Work brought him continuity between one time of his life and another and maybe lessened the loss felt in separation from old friends.

A poem written on an old spinning wheel speaks of the tender relationship between the spinner and the wheel and the changes life brings. Found in the Aurora Spinning Mill's attic by Ron Antoine in the 1980s, the poem was handwritten in German, in pencil, and unsigned:

A Poem of Lament

Old Wheel old loom
Sad victim of progress.
Stored up this loft,
You are left to decay.
How strange does it seem
To find you're so lonely,
A pair of companions
Who had such a sway.

Could those who let the wool move through their fingers, creating textiles to serve others, have sensed that we in the twenty-first century would yearn for connection, continuity, and meaning but often fail to find them in work and everyday life? Perhaps, the poem tells us, craft and community can fill the void.

Their Purpose and Praise

Work in Aurora included music, and the love of music came west with the colony from Bethel. Keil's letters from the overland journey refer to funeral dirges composed and

Pears and apples were turned into fruit butters by the colonists and sold throughout the region. *ACHS photo*

This piccolo book was recently recovered from the basement of a former colony home. The music inside, like the coverlet of this bass and snare drum sheet music, was handcrafted with artistry, though the colonists did not sign their work. Four to five composers have been identified by their distinctive handwriting. Musicians did not note changes on play sheets either; they were expected to learn the work in rehearsals and remember to make corrections as they played. (ACHS collection.) *JK photo*

sung by colonists, and music enjoyed around evening campfires.

Early on, he saw economic potential in the colonists' musical talents. The Bethel Colony Band performed as early as 1847. Aurora's band performed as early as 1856, playing original music, classics, and popular strains like the "Webfoot Quickstep," a seemingly lighthearted acknowledgment of the heavy Willamette Valley rains. Quickly, Aurora provided the de facto state band of Oregon, which played at the Old Settlers' Ball, Willamette and Philomath college graduations, Fourth of July parades in Butteville (as early as 1857), and the Oregon State Fair in 1864. An 1870s newspaper reports the Aurora band would not play at the state fair as previously advertised, as the two-hundred-fifty-dollar fee offered was insufficient. However, the finances must have worked out, as the band performed in following years.

By early 1863, with the influx of new immigrants and skilled musicians from Bethel, the band had grown to thirty-five pieces, including unusual instruments, such as the tuba with dual mouthpieces that allowed sound to be directed forward to an audience or backward while marching. The Pie and Beer Band, later called the Junior Brass Band, was formed for younger men and served as preparation for the larger band. Tycoon Ben Holladay supported the band on a regional tour, sending it by train north to

Puget Sound to promote his railroad, which would eventually have a stop at the Aurora Hotel. Keil received five hundred dollars for the band's services for the communal fund.

Women were not band members but played instruments at home: hammer dulcimers, guitars, zithers, mandolins, eventually pianos, and well-crafted music boxes that were rare and valued. Women did sing in choral groups and with men in mixed choirs; mixed groups may have sung in the wheat fields or while weaving, as both men and women were known to be fine weavers. One can imagine the women singing while walking to the communal wash house or leaving their side of the church on Sunday afternoons. At least one woman was singled out for her vocals: Christina Grob Kraus, who performed solos during colony days.[7]

George Wolfer played the ophicleide, meaning "serpentine" and named for its many twists. A wind instrument on the left leans against the corn shocks, probably colonist-made, as they made many of their own instruments. *ACHS photo.* This Austrian-made cornet used by colonists (right) rests upon needlework (likely made from a punch kit, common throughout the nineteenth century) and unfinished quilt blocks. (10 x 22 inches framed; ACHS collection.) *JK photo*

The 114-foot steeple of the Aurora Colony church, completed in 1867, supported two balconies for the antiphonal concerts by the Aurora Colony Band and other ensembles. A hop field in the foreground makes use of all cropland. *ACHS photo*

Records suggest colony music came from four sources: German, Austrian, and Swiss folk songs passed down orally by descendants, chorales and hymns, original colony compositions, and American patriotic tunes. Several volumes of German folk songs are in the colony collection. Only three old hymnbooks exist; they provide text without music but include suggestions for melodies that would work. These books relate to Lutheran services in the Old Country, where the voices of girls and boys and men and women acted as living examples of the "new song"—"a joyful response to the works of God, stimulated by the Word and the Spirit…sung to God and to each other, with the saints and angels and all creation."[8]

Two balconies wrapped themselves around the church steeple. One held the Aurora band, and the other supported various chamber-music ensembles for when the groups played pieces back and forth antiphonally.

Atop the hotel built in the late 1860s, the flat roof served as another stage for the band to greet visitors arriving on the train. The Park House featured regular concerts of brass cornets, piccolo, tenor horns, tuba, an e-flat three-piston alto horn similar to the baritone horn (it had a mellow tone and was often played as a solo instrument), and the *Schellenbaum* "bell tree."

The Aurora Colony Band, all decked out and ready to help the colony and its visitors celebrate the Fourth of July. Even family pets joined the festivities. *ACHS photos*

An unusual brass instrument, probably manufactured in Paris and played by George Wolfer, was known as an ophicleide, meaning "keyed serpent" for its many twists.

Nonagenarian and descendant Dr. John Keil Richards now conducts a reconstituted Aurora band and repairs such instruments unearthed from descendants' attics. One collection of tubes and bell horns caused quite a challenge in repair, for despite all efforts after reassembly, it would not play. Finally, the maestro peered more closely

The Aurora Colony Band, awaiting passengers they greeted with music, warms up atop the Aurora Hotel. (Note the train tracks in the foreground.) The women would be inside preparing meals. Could they hear the trombone? *ACHS photo*

into a long, slender tube and found, tightly coiled, a magazine picture of a shapely young woman, likely placed there by a young band member to keep it from a mother's prying eyes.

Colony band instructor Henry C. Finck excelled at the violin and guitar, though he could play well and instructed on all instruments, while never accepting payment. Wilhelm Keil played the harmonica but was never known to have joined the band.

Music wove a unique style. Rehearsals were public. Solos had to meet the satisfaction of all musicians present. And performances were dependably harmonious. The colonists seemed to understand that in ancient days, to lose one's temper meant to "go out of tune, to lose *harmonia*,"[9] and they wished to keep the proper balance in all things, on and off stage. Even their popular music and original compositions addressed cultural issues, such as the Civil War, sensitively. Original music performed in repertoire with melodies easily recognizable today, including romantic classics by Beethoven, popular airs by Bellini; and patriotic tunes such as "The Star-Spangled Banner," "Dixie," and "Yankee Doodle. Music was to [the colonists] both a joy and a form of worship."

"The original band pieces, chorales, and songs provided emotional reinforcement to the communal experience at Aurora, offering validity and meaning to the everyday lives of the colonists, and serving as an outward sign of the general contentment."[10]

Though the original compositions left behind were seldom signed—Aurora was a communal society, after all—musicologists are using distinct handwriting and styles to unveil the individuality of the composers, including Wilhelm Keil, Henry C. Finck, Conrad Yost, and Henry C. Ehlen.

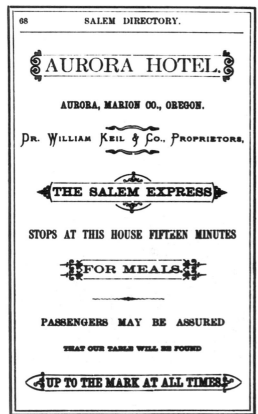

Hotel visitors ate quickly judging by the large meals with only fifteen minutes to savor. *ACHS photo*

Hotel staff, 1880s, at the Aurora Hotel, where Portlanders and others took excursions to consume famed sausage and bread. The cuisine was served first in the hotel and later also at the restaurant colonists built at the Oregon State Fair. *ACHS photo*

"Two young men, Lawrence Ehlen [clarinetist] and William Schwader [cornetist], often came to help us play string quartets," wrote Henry T. Finck, son of the music instructor. "We began with the easy, insipid works of Pleyel, then passed upward to Haydn, Mozart, and Beethoven.… The two young men who played quartets with us were real enthusiasts. Nothing could prevent their coming even when the rain poured down in torrents and their wagon had to be dragged through mud more than a foot deep."[11]

A professor who recalled the band's playing at his own college commencement in 1877, noted their exception skills: "The eighteen members, bearded men of modest mien, were artists, each man upon his favorite instrument. They belonged to that class of early musicians who lived close to nature and drew music from the skies, but were likewise earnest students of the great composers."[12] The group apparently traveled in one of the railroad magnate's stages, swept on the sides with bunting and pulled by six large horses attired with head pompoms and specially decorated harnesses. Dogs, too, tailored for the occasion, trotted alongside. Musicians likely rode atop the stages or held tight to the backboard and waved from inside, a rousing entrance adding to the spectacle of celebration.

Colony compositions accompanied the dances held evenings and Saturday afternoons too. The quadrilles, for example, were slower pieces that gave partners time to talk, then stopped abruptly so dancers could change partners.

The band continued to perform well past the colony period—until the 1920s. Today, a group of exceptional musicians have revived the Aurora Colony Band, this time with both men and women. The youngest is a high-school brass specialist; others include a retired music educator, a professional percussionist using period instruments, a clarinetist with the Oregon Symphony, and artists who play with symphonies in neighboring states.

A Hotel, a Haven, and an Opportunity

The Pioneer Hotel, later known as the Aurora Hotel, with its wide, covered porches, provided more than a place for the band to perform. It offered a variety of working opportunities for Aurora's men and women as a lucrative investment for the colonists. There had been a smaller, stage-stop hotel also known as the Pioneer Hotel; early in the settlement, Keil, who enjoyed visitors and welcomed them to his table, likely served meals to travelers at his *Grosse Haus.*

One woman reported, "My father often went to Aurora prior to the coming of the railroad to partake of those wonderful dinners at the Pioneer Hotel that made Aurora women famous throughout the Northwest and their German dishes spoken of from San Francisco to Victoria."[13]

Once completed in 1867, the Aurora Hotel reached three stories

A contemporary looking tin apple slicer made by a colonist. (ACHS collection.) *NL photo*

into the Oregon sky. Colony-woven coverlets in shades of green, blue, and red, as well as handpieced quilts, would have covered guests' beds. Hospitality would have been a hallmark of anyone's overnight stay. But the hotel's main attraction was food.

Judge Matthew Deady (who later finalized the dissolutions of Aurora and Bethel colonies with great success) wrote in his memoir in 1873: "Went on an evening train with Mrs. D. and Miss Lydia and Henders to Dutchtown. Pleasant ride and evening. At dinner had fried chicken and apple butter. Lydia was astonished and pleased

The Kraus family feeding hungry hogs. Colonists pitched in to raise pigs, render the lard, cure the bacon, and smoke the ham. *ACHS photo*

with everything she saw. After breakfast walked through the orchard and park with Dr. Keil. What a wealth of fruit."[14] On an earlier trip the judge recalled the "sweet milk, apple butter, warm light biscuits, and beef and potatoes fried in the old fashioned way."

In 1874 Charles Nordhoff, a former editor of *Harper's* and the *New York Evening Post,* observed on a visit to Aurora, "On further inquiry I found that I might expect to see there also the best orchards in Oregon, the most ingenious expedients for drying fruits, and an excellent system of agriculture."[15]

The colonists grew abundant gardens, harvesting melons, cabbage, spinach, and tomatoes. Their orchards included apples with names like Newton and Rambo. They might have served salmon in season or huckleberries gathered during a family picnic on the western slopes of Mount Hood. Some of the men hunted wild turkeys and deer; young boys brought down pigeons and grouse. Elk roasts would be served in fall; year-round the colonists raised their own chickens and had plenty of eggs and bacon, sausages, and hams.

They rendered their own lard to flavor breads, pretzels, and piecrusts. On rendering days, everyone participated, helping heat water in brass cauldrons and preparing sausage, sometimes by sewing cloth containers to hold the seasonings and meat when there were insufficient entrails to complete the task. Little from each animal was wasted; a favorite colony saying was, "We used everything but the squeal." Spiced bacon, hams, and sausages hung in smokehouses and sometimes by the hearth for varying lengths of time to bring forth the greatest flavors guests could savor.

"Our 'butcher frolics' were great affairs," one colony member recalled. "Each family had its day when its fat porkers were slaughtered and converted into divers [sic] delicacies."[16]

Visitors and colonists alike savored Aurora cookies, this one from an unknown baker. *ACHS photo*

Not all of this cider was consumed in liquid form. Much of it was boiled in huge kettles all night till most of the water had disappeared as steam, leaving an apple butter which we all relished on bread, especially when, in the last stage, plums or sliced pears had been cooked in with the thickened cider. Aurora apple butter became famous all over the State.

—HENRY T. FINCK, *My Adventures in the Golden Age of Music*

Outsiders enjoyed the millinery skills of colonists. Wooden hangers were handmade by colonists. Note the stylized bird on this Keil-related box.

Henry T. Finck, son of the music instructor, scribed many good words about the Aurora food. A music critic for the *New York Evening Post* and author of several books, he had become in 1876 the first resident of Oregon to graduate from Harvard. His memoir comments on the reasonableness of stagecoaches stopping just twenty-nine miles from Portland: "The trainmen wanted the better meals they could get at Aurora—better meats, better vegetables, better pies and puddings."[17] A hotel sign assured guests of a place to sit and that they'd need only fifteen minutes to partake of the feast provided.

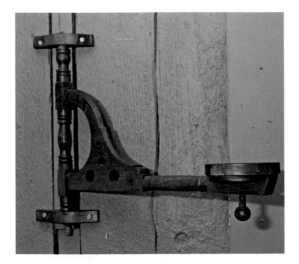

Henry also noted the abundance of crawfish served at family meals and at the hotel. He recalled as a young man in Aurora that they "took the girls along, all were welcome; also we took a pan and salt and matches. When our tin pails were full we killed and cleaned the crawlers—it took some skill to avoid their claws—and made a fire.... I cannot say more for them than that they were as delicious as Chinook salmon."[18]

A candle holder handcrafted by a colonist swings out from the wall, demonstrating practical ingenuity along with fine craftsmanship. (ACHS collection.) *JK photo*

Roly Poly (or, Little Piggy)

This steamed pudding was eaten with rich milk and usually accompanied by a piece of ham or bacon to constitute a full meal. Fresh blackberries in season were used for filling.

Prepare sweet biscuit dough using about 2 cups flour and 1 egg. Divide the dough in half and roll each part into a rectangle 1/2 inch thick. Spread 1 to 1 1/2 cups fresh berries in a layer on the pieces of dough and sprinkle with sugar.

Roll each piece like a jelly roll. Wet two white cloths that are a little larger than the dough.

Wrap the rolls in the cloths and tie the ends with string. Place both rolls in a steamer over boiling water, and steam 1 1/2 to 2 hours until done. Serve warm with rich milk.

—from *Aurora Colony Heritage Recipes*

This contemporary Redwork quilt block by Janus Childs features red embroidery on white cotton. Small original designs such as this pig highlight the block corners. (See page 13; private collection.) *NL photo*

Kraus family members and other colonists harvesting hops. The spindly looking "trees" are hop plants. *ACHS photo*

Several colony women worked at the hotel under the management of Jacob Giesy (not to be confused with the second husband of Emma Giesy), reportedly a hard taskmaster. But the women must have found enjoyment, chatting about an upcoming wedding or progress of a stitching project, exchanging recipes or gossiping about a woman's refusal to share the treasured cooking tip that made her carrot pudding have that special taste. They might have exchanged bluing recipes to keep their caps and aprons such a blinding white.

Katherine Steinbach Becke left one of the few known recipe collections from the Aurora Colony. Her "How to Cook Crawfish" and recipes for Bread Puddings, Bread Tartlets, Vinegar Pie, Buttermilk Pie, and Ginger Cookies are included in the *Aurora Colony Heritage Recipes*. Notations include comments such as, "Better if baked the second day." The crawfish recipe identifies only the seasonings to be added to the water and omits mention of the crawfish.

Women and family pets helped harvest too. This straw cuff, below, worn by men and women (see second woman from right), resembles a thimble. It protected handtailored clothing at harvest and during shop or barn work. *ACHS photo*

Interestingly, Aurora family cookbooks often contained veterinary treatments and home remedies, such as "Treatment for Pink Eye, Cold Cure, Poison Oak" ("wash with buttermilk and soda"), and "Directions for Washing Harness" (from Katherine Steinbach Becke's brown composition book).

The colonists' time cooking at the Oregon State Fair would have cemented the sense of community where music, food, and inventive work culminated. In 1863, the colonists built the first wooden restaurant at the state fairgrounds in Salem, and meals were available twenty-four hours a day. Both men and women cooked and worked in the restaurant, with as many as two hundred colonists spending the entire week in the state capital as the fair grew from two days to more than a week. Their

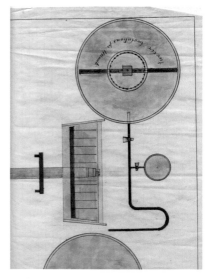

Colonists were engineers who created colorful designs for their work. The distillery sketched and colored here was built in Bethel for the Golden Rule Whiskey the colony made and sold. Once in Aurora, colonists no longer distilled that product, instead marketing pear butter, bands, and beer. *ACHS photos*

efforts brought more visitors other times of the year to their colony's festivals to partake of strawberry shortcakes and Roly Polys; one wonders if colonists understood the French meaning of the word restaurant—"to restore"—and the power of their good meals.

"At the Salem State Fair the meals used to be wretched till an Aurora restaurant was started. It was a huge success from the start. It needed a regular circus tent to accommodate all who crowded in at mealtime; and nearly the whole Aurora Colony, men, women and children, were in Salem for a week, cooking and serving meals."[19]

A narrative of Aurora colony would not be complete without a brief discourse upon the glories of the Aurora table viands. Aurora fried potatoes surpass all other fried potatoes. Aurora home-baked bread is without a peer in this broad land.... Then there were the others dishes. It is doubtful if even the colony descendants can spell their names, so we make no apologies for our attempts in that line. There is stearum, a cross between a pancake and an omelette, fried in a smoking iron pan, difficult to fry, but delightful to partake; there is smearcase, the granddaddy of all cottage cheese; animal cookies, with candy eyes and draped with a sugar that glistens with a luster peculiar to Aurora.

—EDWARD M. MILLER, automobile editor of the *Oregonian*, 1928, quoted in *Aurora Colony Heritage Recipes*

Detail of Triphena Forstner Will's Union Square utility quilt shows purple calico backing, handquilted with thirteen to fifteen stitches per inch. The quilt was hand-pieced with teal and rose colored cotton. (83 x 79 inches; private collection.) *NL photos*

Elizabeth Wolfer and daughter Kate handpieced and handquilted the Peaceful Hours quilt (a variation of the Ohio Star quilt) on display in a typical Sunday-dinner scene at a historic colonist cabin on Old Aurora Colony Museum grounds. The blocks are a variety of calicoes set in muslin and show four different patterns of quilting. Three sides are bound in rust calico; the top is bound in blue. (68 x 82 inches; ACHS collection.) *JK photo*

Entire families camped at the fairgrounds during these October events following harvest, and one wonders if those times reminded some of the overland journey that brought so many colonists so far. Surely, women serving at the fair or the hotel would have heard news of the world and noticed the finery of men and women's clothing, then spread the word to the tailors and seamstresses to meet the latest fashion when a customer from Portland next came their way.

Women's work went beyond creating signature quilts that might take their entire lives or performing everyday piecework necessary for their daughters' petticoats or their children's nightdresses and pants. They churned butter for wooden molds that left impressions of flowers or bird designs when the butter was taken from the mold and put onto a plate. They often sold the beautiful butter to nearby residents of Oregon City or traded for the Buena Vista stone pottery that survives in many descendant households. They taught their daughters how to embroider, appliqué, piece quilts, and cross-stitch, and may have found their greatest comfort with a hoop on their laps, tatting while a child read out loud in the lamplight. The women sewed their clothing and welcomed the arrival of the sewing machine as a more common household item in the mid-1870s. Emma Giesy's 1874 model sewing machine is a part of the Aurora Colony Historical Society collection, and it's believed she must have been one of the best since the colony granted use of special equipment to those most skilled.

The Aurora men made most of the furniture and rugs, buckets, cabinets, bedsteads, baskets, and stools. Men tailored colony clothing and band uniforms and even made the washtubs for cleaning them. They kept a cooper busy creating barrels to store food for shipment, collect rainwater for the dry summer season, and for brewing the ale they made.

Everything related to transportation required a traditional skill from shoeing horses to forming wagon wheels to working leather into harnesses.

Emma Giesy's Wilson sewing machine—the first bought by the colony and given to one of their finest seamstresses in 1874. (ACHS collection.) *NL photo*

Colonist Walt Fry and friend Pat Kelly celebrate potato harvest with their dogs, an Aurora basket, and a corn-cob pipe. *ACHS photo*

George Ehlen's hardware shop served the community. Buggy whips hang from the wall on the right; a picnic is advertised on the chair—for a festive time when work is finished. *ACHS photo*

Gifts they gave at Christmas or birthdays—celebrations requiring cakes, custards, and cottage cheese—all came from their own labor. They harvested herbs and created medicinal treatments, made their own soaps and hair rinses, and dyed the wool they sheared from the sheep that they fed.

Each day would find the colonists knowing that their day's work would be in service to others. Mundane tasks, such as washing, cleaning, and cooking, might wear them down at times, as do these chores today, but their voices would rise in song as they worked together. △

Don't waste life in doubts and fears; spend yourself on the work before you, well assured that the right performance of this hour's duties will be the best preparation for the hours and ages that will follow it.

—RALPH WALDO EMERSON

Tintype, an early form of photography, captured this colony woodworker with the tools of his trade. Finding work to which one was best suited, and work that a community needed, was a virtue sought by the colonists. *ACHS photo*

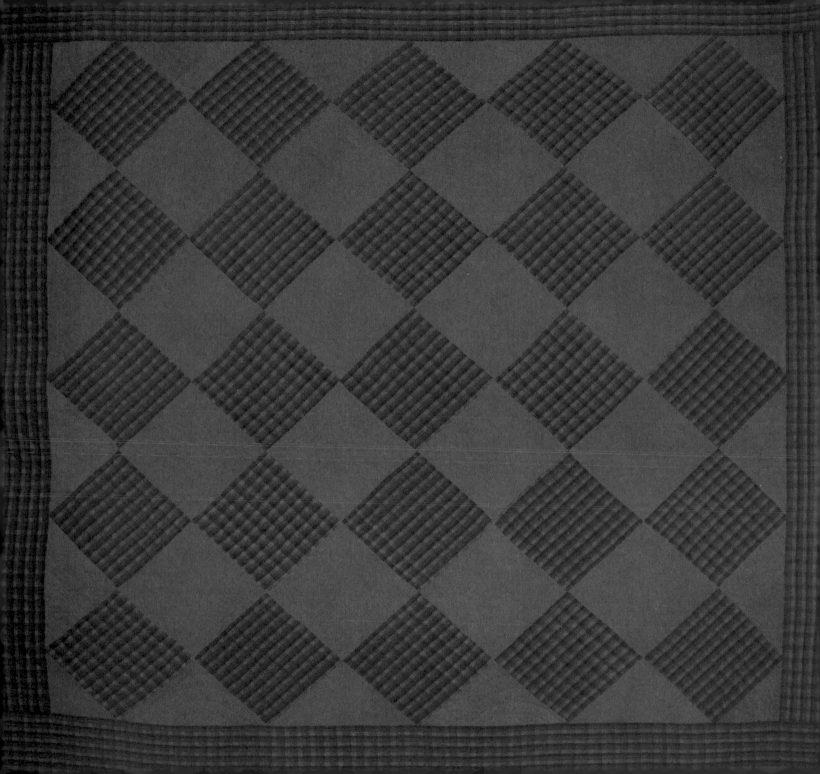

Faith

Their Intense Yearning

A man's life does not consist in the abundance of his possessions.

—LUKE 12:15

A train of 40 wagons with German families arrived at the Dalles
on the 18th. They were bound to Aurora, in this county. The more,
the better, if they are as valuable citizens as those already there.

—*(Salem) Oregon Statesman*, September 28, 1863

As they had in Bethel, Christmas celebrations began at 4 a.m. in Aurora. Church bells rang across the Pudding
River to the hills and swales of the village where people gathered, their shawls and coverlets pulled tight against frosty air.
Some wore woolen caps tied beneath their chins. Quilted petticoats warmed stockinged legs under women's heavy skirts. A
trumpet sounded and families followed the band up the hill. Close behind the tubas walked young girls carrying lighted

Emma Wagner Giesy's Running Squares on Point, circa 1850–60, 79 x 81 inches

Detail of Emma's Running Squares on Point: backing is colony woven red and blue plaid. The wool was grown, washed, dyed, carded, spun, and woven in a much-used pattern typical of the colony at both its Bethel and Aurora mills. Dyes were natural. *NL photo*

candles to place within a large star frame inside the church. The *Schellenbaum*, handcrafted by John Bauer back in Bethel, was carried like a flag by a band member, then placed in its standard near the front, heat from the candles and a draft in the room moving the clappers and jingling tiny bells.

Men and women entered through separate side entrances but sang together traditional songs brought with them from Europe. They raised their voices in chorales that dated from the sixteenth century.

The colonists followed their own unique form of Christianity as seekers, people longing to create something different and new as they served God. The German word *Sehnsucht* means "intense yearning" (*sehn,* "to long for," and *sucht,* "like a mania"). Hadn't such longing brought them west? Letters from colonists to family and friends answer yes, indeed, *Sehnsucht* was found in the community of Aurora.

Following the Christmas morning sermon by Dr. Keil—or, at his invitation in the 1870s, speaking by some of the younger men—the band played yet again and huge baskets of cakes, apples, cookies, and candied pumpkins were distributed to the children. A communal meal followed with hams, sausages, cakes, pies, and surely sauerkraut made fresh from cabbages buried the previous fall within fresh-mown hay. Chatter and laughter rose to the thick-beamed rafters.

These festivities were some of the rare times when young men and women associated together outside of shared work and music festivals, and it happened in the safety of the church. The colonists celebrated the entire day, eating and dancing. Family gift giving occurred either on Christmas Eve or later on Christmas Day; celebrations went on through the week into the new year, marking Christmas and Epiphany, or Twelfth Day, high holidays of the colony's religious calendar. Only Easter and the celebrations for Wilhelm and Louisa Keil's shared March birthdays are remembered as well as Christmas festivities.

To celebrate Christ's resurrection, Easter was a day of great importance in which colonists colored eggs and scratched them with designs. They gave gifts as they'd done in Pennsylvania and Missouri, and they worshiped at the hilltop church with the band playing on the outside terraces.

Worship through the year, every other Sunday, still held pageantry. Labor often stopped on Saturday at noon for eating and coming together, with worship on Sunday as a daylong gathering. One can imagine the sliced venison and potato salad carried up the hill in towel-covered baskets and the Sunday aprons covering dresses of linen, wool, pink and white Sea Mist calico, a favorite pale blue dotted cloth that decades later appeared in many pieced quilts.

As with most of the communal societies of the nineteenth century, the pin holding everything together was the leader. Keil, born in Prussia in 1812, had left Germany for Pennsylvania in the 1830s during a religious time known as the Second Great Awakening. Revival preachers and evangelists moved across the continent, urging religious devotion and faith as the means of settling the fears of unsettling times. Most of these preachers

Apples still grow on trees planted circa 1860s by colonists. Old trees need old-timers to tend them.

Interior of the 1867 Aurora colony church. Each column was turned from a single log. The spare and splendid pulpit rested only two steps above the congregants, unlike many high and removed altars of the period. The church took three years to build, as skilled artisans needed to arrive from Bethel. *ACHS photo*

emphasized plain living and personal religious experience not mediated by the church. Scholars believe Keil followed a German Methodist revivalist, Wilhelm Nast, who led the young man through "an emotional experience of guilt about his former way of life [when he had dabbled in mysticism], experienced exhilarating relief over being forgiven those transgressions, and developed a passionate desire and commitment to live a new, holy life."[1]

In 1838, Keil began leading revivalist meetings in people's homes, praying

and exhorting them to repentance and singing hymns of praise, actions not out of the ordinary for preachers of the time. He began to resist controls of the German Methodist Church and, in particular, disliked the idea that preachers received a salary. Instead he preferred to live "all things in common," every man according to his need. Present-day Christians might say Keil wished congregants and preachers to live by faith, assured that God provides; this view is chronicled by several samplers in the colony collection.

The old colony church. Women entered from one side; men from the other. Worship began on Saturday afternoon with music and dancing. On Sundays, Keil, and later other chosen men, delivered a message from Scripture, followed by a feast. The church was dismantled in 1911. *ACHS photo*

Keil gained followers who came with him to the Protestant Methodist Church and then followed him again when he left. He continued to reject "paid clergy, the narrowness of denominations, and the regulatory practices of religious bodies."[2] His preaching continued in revivalist mode, exhorting listeners that the route to a contented life was to repent, convert, and practice holy living. Keil soon designated missionaries to bring more people to this repentance, conversion, and state of grace demonstrated by simple, faithful living.

Christian Giesy was one of these early missionaries, long before he was sent west in 1853 with his wife, Emma, and eight other scouts. Christian brought into the fold men who later played important roles in the colony, such as professors Karl Ruge and Christopher Wolff, the former Lutheran pastor.

The 1840s began a time of seeking, questioning, and changing religious persuasions. Those writing about Keil describe a change in his preaching. He began leaning on the Old Testament book of Daniel and the New Testament text of Revelation. Both explored "end times," a common theme among revivalists. As many followers of another revivalist (who had predicted the world's end) left to join

the Shaker community, Wolff and Keil began shaping their own dream: communal living with shared labor and arts as a response to the corrupt world. Several families, including the Wagners and Wolfers, had left George Rapp's communal society seeking a new leader and finding it in Keil.

Recruits were now sent, not to bring in converts to the Pennsylvania community but to find property in Missouri for Keil's communal hope. Bethel was formed.

Holy living continued to be preached there, and members worked to create the perfect community, replacing selfish individualism with love and healing. Key components that Keil brought with him to Aurora nearly ten years later were living unselfishly and realizing the Golden Rule of doing unto others as you would have others do unto you. Aurora colonists went further and described a Diamond Rule: the desire to make another's life better than one's own. Both of these rules were demonstrated by a willingness to provide shelter, medicine, and food for those in need, even those outside the colony—and this commitment, in part, is what allowed Dr. Keil to permit a colonist to help an outside family afflicted with smallpox, and likely led to the eventual exposure and death of four of his own children.

Union Square quilt, shown with handmade colony basket, machine-pieced between 1860 and 1888 by Emma Wagner Giesy, on display in the Frederick Keil home. With ten stitches to the inch, Emma handquilted the feather design in a diagonal line at the border with stems and leaves in each corner. (83 x 84 inches; ACHS collection.)
JK photo

Supports of a Three-Legged Stool

Three dominant themes mark the colony's faith practices, according to University of Missouri professor of religion David Nelson Duke.

First, Keil kept Aurora a place of safety for his flock. Corruption of the outside world would be contended through God's protection and their brotherhood. *Gott mit uns* ("God with us") was said to be the colony's motto and indeed appears as Redwork and in cross-stitched samplers. Keil's letters during this time speak of God's people working against the forces of evil, and he may have preached this often on Sundays to unite the colonists and remind them of their choice to live differently while building a new life and village.

Crown of Thorns by Triphena Forstner Will. Machine-pieced, the handquilting features a detailed sawtooth border of pink on white cotton. (Circa 1890–1910; 78 x 78 inches; private collection.) *JC photo*

Second, Keil's unchallenged charismatic leadership influenced everything. Charismatic leaders often fail to train or prepare for their own deaths so that followers can carry on, and Keil fit this category. He never claimed to be a prophet like his contemporary Joseph Smith, nor any kind of deity. Instead Keil relied on God and his interpretations of the Bible. But he was patriarchal. Colonists often called him Father. One of the tenets of the Articles of Agreement states that the society should be modeled on the family with Keil as leader and "autocrat," whose word was law. A woman's view held little sway in this society. (However, certain women—for one, Helena Giesy, sister to John, Christian, and Andrew—were revered for their devotion and faithfulness to the community.) He was also confrontational about indiscretions and said to berate colonists in front of other members of the "family," for their own good and as community examples. Descendants have passed down a taut memory of Keil publicly chastising a Will family member because Mr. Will had rejected Keil's methods for healing his weakened arm.

The third theme is the compassion and care for one's neighbors, the hallmark that allowed colonists to weave their way into the outside villages and towns as a people admired not only for their quality of craft but for their generosity of spirit. In Aurora, no one was left wanting. Orphans, widows, the frail and elderly, all knew safe harbor.[3]

Detail of Crown of Thorns quilt.

An 1844 document detailing the communal views of the Bethel society begins, "This society must not rest on anything else than the love of God, so that every opportunity for selfish gain be excluded.... The purpose of this society is not to lay up treasures, but to administer continuously help to the poor, and in this we base ourselves on the Word of God: 'Having therefore food and raiment let us be content.'"[4]

The gold and silver silk threading in this "Trust in God for Every Need" sampler suggests the influence of European guilds on styles for ecclesiastical subjects. The maker is not known, but the sentiment was a hallmark of the Bethel, Willapa, and Aurora colonies. This sampler came from Bethel, Missouri, arriving in Aurora in the 1980s. (18.5 x 14.5 inches framed; ACHS collection.) *JK photo*

Even if people left the colony, which they were allowed to do at any time, compassion prevailed. "But should one or another brother be no longer willing to remain with us, the Word of God also says: 'You shall not let your brother go away from you empty.' Thus, in this matter also, we shall find a way to deal with the brother, that we might abide in love."[5]

The colonists believed Aurora was created in the image of God's family. A strong, loving Father designed their world, and his guidance and personal care could be counted on in times of trial. They relied on Scripture and had family Bibles from which they read both in times of trouble and to celebrate contentment. With God, they trusted that all their storms would be but small squalls.

So why, when faith was such an obvious foundation to their community, did colonists meet only every other Sunday? And why didn't they celebrate the sacrament of communion or were there no mentions of baptisms? Members of other denominations in the region (Methodists, Catholics, Presbyterians, Congregationalists, Mennonites) worshiped weekly, and baptisms were definitely Lutheran expressions of faith.

Descendants say Keil did speak of communion following each service, how at that Last Supper Christ

The Colony Articles of Agreement—1867

1. All government should be parental, to imitate the parental government of God.

2. Societies should be formed on the model of the family.

3. All interests and all property are kept absolutely in common.

4. Members labor faithfully for the general welfare and support.

5. The means of living is drawn from the general treasury.

6. Neither religion nor the harmony of nature teaches community in nothing further than property and labor.

7. The family is strictly maintained; people marry, raise and train children.

8. Each family has its own house, or separate apartments, in one of the large buildings.

9. The children of the Community are sent to school, open year-round.

10. Dr. Keil is president and autocrat. He has selected advisors to assist in the management of affairs. When vitally important changes or experiment is contemplated, nothing is done without the general consent of the community.

11. Plain living and rigid economy are inculcated as duties from each to the whole: Labor regularly and waste nothing. Each workshop has a foreman. The fittest comes to the front. Men shall not be confined to one kind of labor. If brick masons are needed and the shoemaker is not busy, the shoemaker makes brick.

Yarn sampler completed by one of the Wagner girls. The sentiment expresses the colonists' desires to preserve the story of the colony and its people, as they sought a unique American experience of brotherhood, compassion, and service. (21 x 8.5 inches framed; private collection.) *JK photo*

gathered his followers to break bread, to ask that they remember him, and to support one another in trying times ahead. But perhaps Keil wanted to avoid the pitfalls of doctrine and legalistic demands that marked the European church in the eighteenth century. A rebellion against these dogmatic excesses is what brought him and many of the colonists to America in the first place. Maybe he determined that worshiping every other Sunday, beginning with a festive meal and ending with dancing on Sunday evenings, distinguished the colony in an individualistic way.

Whatever the reason, assembly days were an important part of colony life, and there is evidence the colonists attempted daily to live their faith through relationships, craft, and work.

The First Church Building

Though schools and churches were often the first buildings constructed in other frontier towns, Aurora did not build its house of worship until later. Colonists met on the upper floor of Keil's

Detail of a contemporary Redwork quilt, featuring one of the familiar colony mottoes. (Private collection.) The facing page shows the colony repair shop. Colonists made most of their own furniture, looms, and spinning wheels—and the tools for making repairs themselves. The work of their hands demonstrated their faith. Note the yarn winder or "weasel" near the hoops hanging on the wall. Such weasels inspired the children's song "Pop Goes the Weasel." (ACHS collection.) *JK photos*

Top of window from Aurora Colony Church, 1867. *JK photo*

Grosse Haus for worship. It's likely that Keil needed essential craftsmen to build and furnish the church building in the way he had in mind, forcing him to wait for particular Bethel arrivals. Or perhaps meeting in a home was reminiscent of the first-century house churches where families and neighbors gathered to sustain the faith.

After three years of construction and following the last of the mass migrations out of Bethel, the Aurora church was dedicated in 1867. The steeple rose 114 feet, the highest point of the village, toward the heavens. Musical chimes were installed, and bells, ordered from Ohio and transported around the South American horn, were brought up the Columbia and Willamette rivers, then with great effort overland to Aurora. Hendricks describes "rose windows" in the church in his book about Aurora, but the top of the otherwise rectangular window that survives forms a gothic arch within an arch. There were two of these tall windows behind the altar, similar to those that lined the sides. Pictures show four long windows along each side of the church, with doors at the center walls for separate men's and women's entrances.

Colony craftsmen turned the long pillars that marched down both sides of the interior and supported the upper choir loft in the back. A woodstove at the center back offered heat. Pews of single boards of lumber, twenty-two feet long, rested in rows on either side of a center aisle. In 1911, the building was dismantled and the pews were removed. Several are now used in the Aurora Presbyterian Church across from the Oxbarn Museum.

A Theology of Service

Keil's theology was expressed within the foundation of the colony. He urged brotherly love, meeting needs communally, and creating an active community that served and enjoyed the abundance of a faithful life while permitting artistry and craftsmanship, beauty and utility, and a sense of joy.

Children were important in Aurora. Keil gave them fruits and danced with youngsters at the annual March party in the great hall when the colony celebrated the birthdays of both Keil and his wife, Louisa. It's said that after dancing with the children—their leather shoes resting on his toes—Keil and the children retired to the sidelines as the elders then enjoyed themselves with polkas and quicksteps through the night. One wonders if mothers helped the older children put the little ones to sleep on the floor in the back of the hall, covering them with coverlets of red, green, and the Aurora blue.

It's said that Keil's sermons were engaging and inspiring. He often quoted phrases from the Bible:

- "Thou shalt not covet."
- "As every man hath received the gift, even so minister the same one to another."
- "This commandment we have from Him, that he who loveth God, love his brother also."

Other samplers in the colony collection include short religious admonishments or encouragements:

- In God We Trust
- From each according to his ability / To each according to his need.
- God With Us

Note the stylized window in the barn, believed to be from the church. *ACHS photo*

Keil's Leadership

While Keil held the people together with his charismatic words and communal practices, he also cast piercing, judging eyes and quoted scriptures that did not comfort. Many described his view on the death of a child as bearing witness to "sins of the fathers" rather than smallpox or fevers.

Keil described the death of his own son, Willie, as a necessary sacrifice God called him to make for the good of the colony.[6] He must have struggled with an explanation six years later when four more of his children died of smallpox within days of one another. Their loss brought about profound grieving. Descendant accounts say Keil isolated himself from the colony and allowed others to make decisions, preach, and distribute medicines. One descendant reported that Keil was so removed, people had to remind him that they had come all the way from Bethel "to be with you," urging him to reengage in the community. He eventually did; the colonists held fast to their communal spirit.

But the community was not to last.

Christopher Wolff, a deputy president designated in the mid-1860s, tried desperately to have Keil think about how the communal society could continue upon his death. Some say Wolff saw Aurora as an oasis of education and creativity that would dwindle away without the singular

The Cookie Cutter quilt, handappliquéd and hand-dyed, is named for the tin cookie cutter colonists used as a template to create the bird motif in the four corners. Made by an unknown quilter of the Wolfer-Scholl family, the sunflower or hexlike pattern was typical among German folk artists of Pennsylvania. Featured are twelve appliquéd tulip baskets and a splendid eight-inch border of appliquéd grapevines and grape bunches, each with twenty-one grapes. Double quilted, with fifteen stitches per inch, this was considered a life project quilt. Detail of the Cookie Cutter quilt is shown at right. (Circa 1870; 96 x 80 inches; ACHS collection.) *JK photos*

leadership of Keil. Hendricks wrote that Keil did not respond to Wolff's constant urging and that it caused a rift between the men. Still, Wolff remained in the colony and was there when Keil died.[7]

In the end, Wolff was correct. Within two years of Keil's death in 1877, the two colonies that had survived for more than forty years disbanded with assets distributed to both men and women:

> Many…colonist still recall the community day with serene pleasure…. The association of kindred spirits, the freedom, the ease they enjoyed, the absence of care and responsibility, the fraternal feeling and the devotion to a common cause…. The old bond of fellowship still existed…. Community life seems not to have unfitted the members for the struggle in individualism…. All of them are doing well at some trade or profession."[8]

Jake Ritter enjoys a moment of play and rest with his wife, Kate, as colonists would on Sundays. Wrapped in a Nine Patch infant quilt (also called Bear Paw), Kate traveled in the arms of her mother, Elizabeth Wolfer Zimmerman, who walked beside the family wagon from Bethel, Missouri, to Aurora, Oregon, in 1863. The Zimmermans ran Aurora's tannery "a far piece" from the village. *ACHS photo*

One must marvel at their efficiency and cooperation. At the time of dissolution following Keil's death, the colonists from Bethel and Aurora worked out details so that Judge Deady had little to do but finalize the results. A great portion of property in Bethel and Aurora was, in fact, still in Keil's name only and thus descended to his wife and son; both relinquished any ownership and requested that divisions be made equitably among the colonists. Not a single lawsuit was lodged against the final outcome, despite two colonies, the interests of people in three states, and values of property estimated at more than one hundred thousand dollars.[9] How remarkable this is compared to today, when even in small families following the death of a loved one, squabbles over property can go on for years.

Historian William Bek suggests that long after the dissolution, many colonists continued to live in harmony with neighbors and on the farmsteads and in colony houses their families built. They still gathered on winter afternoons to stitch and weave or work a harness, and they moved into the individualistic economic world buttressed by the landscape, relationships, work, and faith that had built and sustained their lives for more than twenty years.

A sampler stitched by Rosanna Stauffer, one of the aunties who helped raise baby Matilda after the death of her mother, Matilda Knight Stauffer (creator of the Sunflower quilt featured on page 8), and her twin, in 1867. (30 x 28.5 inches framed; ACHS collection.) *JK photo*

Their legacy includes artifacts marked with individuality, beauty, and unique design as they contributed to community; descendants who also became artists and craftsman, choosing careers in pharmacy, medicine, music, and writing; and a place of refuge marked by gentleness, hope, devotion, abundance, and brotherly love.

In our celebrity-focused culture, some believe only extraordinary stories are worthy of immortalizing. But the colonists demonstrate that even simple, ordinary lives shape meaning long after the century in which they lived. Their experiences are told through quilt, community, and craft, and the beauty reminds us of the value in remembering both the spare and the splendid in our lives.

Whig's Defeat Variation quilt by Triphena Forstner Will. Handpieced appliqué, handquilted, ten to twelve stitches per inch, in double lines common to the colony. Quilting designs include Prairie Points, half- and quarter-feather wreaths, crosshatching, flowers, fan, and in the border, an alternating diagonal pattern. Notice the fine buttonhole stitches at the edge of the tulips in the detail above. (Circa 1890; 89 x 89 inches; private collection.) *JK photos*

You, Too, Can Leave a Legacy

While the colony disbanded officially in 1883, its richness continues under the tender auspices of the Aurora Colony Historical Society and Museum, its many volunteers, and colony descendants. Changing exhibits, children's programs, and community festivals at the Stauffer-Will farmstead remind us that we, too, will leave a legacy. How that legacy is interpreted can be enhanced through simple actions honored today. Our lives are the stories others read first.

- **Tell a story** how a treasure, like a wooden duck decoy or pieced quilt, came into your family's possession. A silversmith I knew did this about books he wanted to give his wife and two daughters and why he'd chosen each title. He wrote his story on a 2 x 3 inch motel notepad and brought the women in his life to tears with his brief expressions of how uniquely he knew each of them.

- **Make notes in a family recipe book.** "This was Mom's favorite. She used apple cider vinegar only." Notes about a loved one's practice are irreplaceable.

- **Make quilts or wall hangings** from your father's ties, mother's dresses, or son's favorite T-shirts. How-to books abound on ways for textiles to record family histories.

- **Jot down the date, place, and names of people in photographs.** A sentence or two describing the occasion fills in gaps that memory or facts cannot.

- **Write a New Year's letter** to a yet-unborn great-great-grandchild about something that marks your family. For example: "We were dairy farmers," and, "She was the first in our family to graduate from high school." Or, "He broke horses for the cavalry," and, "We dug for clams on Willapa Bay." Include birth stories and family traditions, and mention special artifacts, crafts, and textiles handed down.

- **Make simple notes on an almanac calendar,** as did many nineteenth-century women who had no time for journal writing. For instance: "January 1: Missy gave birth to foal we named Buck." And, "March 20: Chickens laying again. Got six eggs today." This kind of record won't disappear into cyberspace and can bring alive a time past. Tell family members you've recorded these memories and where they're stored; if you're fortunate to discover such calendars among family artifacts, read them at least once and consider donating them to local historical societies.

- **Make a family tree, and remember to trace the women.** Unfortunately, too many women's histories are forgotten, not recorded, or overlooked; too many family trees miss important branches because daughters' lines haven't been traced. Yet women's lives often reflect the everyday events of parenting and keeping the hearth. Cherishing their stories is an important part of the American experience. One colony descendant shared surprise and delight upon learning in my novels that Emma Giesy had two sons *and* two daughters, as she'd only heard stories of the boys.
- **Record, digitize, and preserve** old photographs and family stories. Commercial photographic companies and online services can restore yellowed, faded, and torn photographs or slides and place them on CDs. Even pulling pictures with sentiments from albums and placing them in photographic activity tested (PAT) plastic folders helps preservation. Meanwhile, encourage Grandma to tell her stories and videotape them; tell your own stories this way too. Have a photo day and digitally photograph *your* heirlooms, labeling the pictures and making CD copies to share with siblings or children. Encourage them to do the same so that precious artifacts with meaning don't end up in a garage or estate sale, lost to the family forever.
- **Volunteer at and support state and local museums,** or become involved in groups devoted to helping people write and research family stories, or genealogical societies, passionate about discovering and recording family journeys. Such involvement models for children the importance of history in helping build the future. As Aurora Colony Historical Society member Brian Asher once noted, children cannot teach themselves about the past—we have to do it for them.

This colony-built Octagon House was near the railroad, but its purpose is unclear because no one told its story. Do you know what such structures were used for? Help the colony find this legacy, and let it be a reminder to write your own. (ACHS collection.) *JK photo*

Two Colony Quilts

Patterns and Instruction for You to Replicate

The Bay Leaf Quilt

The Bay Leaf pattern, known to some as Orange Peel, demonstrates the geometric shapes and forms found in many colony quilts and that the colonists used as a contemporary design. Distinct to Aurora are the extraordinary colors and varied shapes. See the vibrant purples and reds in the Bay Leaf quilt pictured on page 134.

For best results, read all instructions before beginning. Please note that this project is for an experienced quilter. Instructions replicate how Aurora quilters would have created this project, but modern techniques may be used. All measurements include a quarter-inch seam allowance.

The finished quilt top for this replica is 32 x 32 inches. While the colony quilt was handstitched, this replica was machine quilted. This replica also differs from the original because the points of the central shape extend beyond the center circle and match where the blocks come together.

Fabrics and Supplies

This quilt, a reproduction of a circa 1850 original, is made using 100 percent cotton fabrics. The original quilt was made from wool, with a pieced back.

- 1 yard of background fabric
- 1 yard of fabric for center pieces
- 1/2 yard each of two fabrics for bay leaf shapes
- 1/4 yard of fabric for binding
- 1 yard of fabric or a variety of scraps for the backing

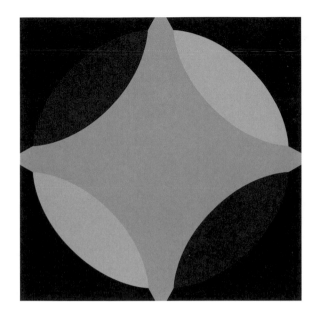

Next, cut one 17-inch square per block of the background fabric; the sample is made from four blocks. The gray form in the center of the block is finished at 15 inches.

Piecing the Blocks

Machine stitch the four bay leaf pieces to the center piece. Before pressing, clip the curved seams. Next, center the pieced block onto the background fabric, then hand appliqué, using a needle-turn technique. Start and end machine stitching one quarter inch from the ends of the bay leaf so edges can be turned under for appliquéing.

Cutting

Annette James, a quilter in Aurora and a board member at the Aurora Colony Historical Society, contributed these patterns. She commented, "Having to make my own pattern was a challenge, so I thought about what quilters of this time period might have used. I found a mixing bowl in the perfect circle size, so it was my pattern." Take the pattern above to be photocopied and enlarged, then cut it apart for your pattern, starting with a 15½ inch circle. Place the tissue bay leaf piece over your material to cut your fabric pieces. Annette said, "I chose three different fabrics for the play on design."

This Bay Leaf quilt (with colony-made baskets), also known as Orange Peel, by Emily Giesy Miller (circa 1880–1910; 61 x 70.5 inches; ACHS collection), is made of red and purple wool in a bold original design. Annette James, replica quilter, and Elizabeth Corley made the replica pattern. *JK photo*

Assembling the Quilt Top

Square up the blocks so that all are the same size before sewing the four blocks together using a quarter-inch seam. Press.

Quilting and Finishing

Cut a batting several inches larger than the quilt top. Lay the backing on a flat surface, wrong side up. Secure the edges with tape. Position the batting over the backing, smoothing it flat. Position the quilt top on the batting. Hand-baste or safety-pin the layers together. Trim the batting and the backing even with, or a quarter-inch beyond, the edges of the quilt. Colony quilters often used the feather wreath quilting pattern.

Binding

The binding for quilts can be cut either on the bias or on the straight of grain. You may join many pieces of fabric with diagonal seams to make one continuous binding strip 136 x 2½ inches. Apply binding in your preferred method.

The Nine Patch Double-Sided Quilt

A Nine Patch reversible quilt wrapped a young colonist who was carried in her mother's arms across the prairie from Missouri to Oregon. The Nine Patch was typical of colony quilts thought to be especially useful because of its reversible pattern—and because it was made from pieces of old shirts, pants, or whatever was available. It has a sturdy, scrappy sense of creativity, but colors would likely vary from darker to bright, if the material was available.

The finished quilt top for this replica is 26 x 26 inches. For best results read all instructions before beginning. Use quarter-inch seams throughout. All measurements include this quarter-inch seam allowance.

Fabrics and Supplies

This quilt is made of 100 percent cotton homespun and flannel fabrics. Using a variety of fabrics gives the scrappy look that's authentic to many original quilts of this pattern; leftover fabrics from others projects or fat quarters work nicely. (Fat quarters are useful cuts of fabric created from a half yard of a 44-inch-wide fabric. Cut that piece in half to get an 18 x 22 inch piece of fabric or a fat quarter.)

Cutting for the Blocks

Each nine-patch block contains five squares of one fabric and four squares of a contrasting fabric, so you will need:

- 90 squares, each $2^{1}/_{2}$ x $2^{1}/_{2}$ inches in combinations of your choice

Plain Blocks (not pieced)
- 8 blocks, each $6^{1}/_{2}$ x $6^{1}/_{2}$ inches

Inside Border
- 4 strips of $17^{1}/_{2}$ x $1^{1}/_{2}$ inches
- 4 strips of 20 x $1^{1}/_{2}$ inches

Outside Border
- 4 strips of 20 x $3^{1}/_{2}$ inches
- 4 strips of 26 x $3^{1}/_{2}$ inches

Piecing the Blocks

Lay out the blocks as in the diagram below. Using a scant quarter-inch seam allowance, sew three horizontal rows of squares. Press seams toward the darker fabric. Join the rows and press. Nine-patch blocks should measure $6^{1}/_{2}$ x $6^{1}/_{2}$ inches. Make a total of ten nine-patch blocks. Press.

Assembling the Quilt Top

Now lay out the blocks as shown. You will need two groupings, one for each side of the quilt. Using a scant quarter-inch seam allowance, sew three horizontal rows of blocks. Join the rows and press.

Inner Border

Sew a 17¹/₂ x 1¹/₂ inch inner border to the sides of the quilt. Now sew a 20 x 1¹/₂ inch inner border to the top and bottom edges of the quilt. You will need to do this for the front and the back.

Outer Border

Sew a 20 inch outer border to the sides of the quilt. Now sew a 26 inch outer border to the top and bottom of the quilt. You will need to do this for the front and the back.

Quilting and Finishing

Cut the batting several inches larger than the quilt top. Lay the pieced back on a flat surface with the wrong side up. Secure the edges with tape. Center the batting over the backing, smoothing it flat. Position the quilt top on the batting.

At this point you will need to line up the bottom and top nine-patches. Take a straight pin and, pushing it through the corner of one block, pass it through the batting and into the same corner on the back. Repeat this process several times, lining up all the blocks.

Hand-baste or safety-pin the layers together. Trim the batting and the bottom nine-patch even with or a quarter inch beyond the edges of the quilt top.

The Nine Patch double-sided quilt was hand quilted using a primitive stitch. Stitch about four to five stitches to the inch using regular quilting thread or a pearl cotton, which gives a nice texture to the quilt. Contemporary quilters may use timesaving methods to make this Nine Patch.

This double-sided Nine Patch quilt was made by a member of the Wolfer-Scholl family (circa 1870–1890; 58 x 78 inches; ACHS collection), using a combination of machine and hand-woven wool fabrics. All handstitched and quilted in a crosshatched pattern, four to five stitches per inch. Annette James, replica quilter, and Joan Jacobs made the replica pattern. *JK photo*

Binding

The binding for many old quilts is cut on the straight of grain. You may join many pieces of fabric with diagonal seams to make one continuous binding strip of 106 x 2½ inches. Sew the binding flush to the edge of the quilt, batting, and backing, using the quarter-inch seam. Then turn the binding over the edge, covering the seam, and hand sew down. Enjoy!

Acknowledgments

The author and Aurora Colony Historical Society wish to thank the many descendants of colony families for their contributions, especially for allowing us to photograph artifacts and for sharing their stories. Many opened their homes to us, took us into bedrooms and attics and cellars, and answered dozens of questions. They are named here without attachment to a particular artifact in order to protect their privacy and the anonymity of places where their artifacts are preciously kept: Steve and Rhetta Braun, Diane Kocher Downs, Marie Kocher Hall, Louise Hankenson, Gary and Elaine Ihle, Dr. Jerry and Barbara Giesy, Terri Roberts of the Anna Becke House Bed and Breakfast, Dorothy and Byron Schriever, Michael L. Truman, Vera Yoder, Dr. David G. and Patricia Wagner, and scores of others who shared their artifacts and stories for the society's exhibits and publications through the years.

Thanks to Brian Asher, Jim and Sue Kopp, John Holley, Norm Bauer (who first suggested to me a quilt book that I expanded into all crafts), Gail Robinson, Gary Ihle, Bob Higgins, Andrew Willet, Blaine Schmeer, Roberta Hutton, and former director John Holley of the society for their trust, insight, generosity, hard work, and direction. In addition, thanks to Aurora tour guide Janus Childs for her photographic expertise and for the use of her Redwork pieces as part of this project.

I'm grateful to John Sherrill Houser for writing the gracious prelude to this book. He spent time in Aurora as a child, and his artistry today still exemplifies the exceptional qualities for which the colonists were so known.

To Sandra Dallas, Mary Bywater Cross, and Stephanie Grace Whitson, I extend my admiration for their own storytelling through quilts and my gratitude for their encouragement that I could tell the Aurora story even though I wasn't a quilter myself.

Thanks as well go to Pendleton Woolen Mills for generously providing the woolen fabric for the replica of Emma Giesy's quilt to be given away in a drawing for a colony quilt. Readers can participate in that drawing by visiting WaterBrookPress.com and clicking on Contests or by sending a self-addressed, stamped envelope to Contests, WaterBrook Multnomah Publishing Group, 12265 Oracle Boulevard, Suite 200, Colorado Springs, Colorado, 80921.

The fine team at WaterBrook Multnomah Publishing Group undertook this project and saw it through with their usual care for quality. Special praise goes to editor Jeanette Thomason for championing the remarkable nature of the colony artifacts and story, to Karen Sherry and the design team, and to the marketing, sales, and publicity teams who made this book an artifact all its own. And to Laura Wright, my eternal gratitude.

Gratitude beyond words goes to Nancy Lloyd not only for her photographic skills but her assistance in the duration of this project, organizing and sorting more than a thousand photographs, scanning hundreds of historical photographs, and for the ten days spent with us on Starvation Lane, enduring her allergies to dogs and helping me put the photographs and manuscript into some semblance of a draft book. This project could not have happened without her.

Words pale as well in thanking society curator Patrick J. Harris; quilt curator, board member, and volunteer extraordinaire Annette James; staff members Janus Childs, Elizabeth Corley, and Pam Weninger; and volunteer archivist Irene Westwood. Without their expertise and enthusiasm this story would not have been told through quilts, community, and crafts. I will be forever grateful.

I thank my husband, Jerry, for his hours of photographic work, his patience as always with my effort to tell stories, and for his unwavering faith in me. That we're still married after the photographing of this project speaks volumes about his tolerance of and care for me these past thirty-two years. I love you more than all the gravel in the John Day River.

Finally, I thank my readers, who since 1991 have shown constant interest in and support for my bringing historical stories to life and who have listened to the voices of the past and what they have to tell us.

From left: volunteer photographer and assistant Nancy Lloyd, ACHS quilt consultant Annette James, and ACHS curator Patrick Harris hard at work keeping the past of Aurora constantly present. *JK photo*

Notes

Epigraph. Russell Blankenship, *And There Were Men* (New York: Knopf, 1942), 93–94.

Epigraph. Elizabeth Zimmerman to "Dear Aunt Mary Zimmerman" in Hubbard, Oregon, quoted in *Stitched in Time: Thirty-Fourth Annual Quilt Show* (Aurora, OR: Aurora Colony Historical Society, 2006).

Part 1: Craft

Epigraph. Former president Jimmy Carter, quoted in Jo Lauria and Steve Fenton, *Craft in America* (New York: Clarkson Potter, 2007), 10.

1. Alan Guggenheim, *Oregon Music Project* grant application (Aurora, OR: Aurora Colony Historical Society, 2005).

Part 2: Landscape

Epigraph. Rainer Maria Rilke, *Rilke's Book of Hours: Love Poems to God,* trans. Anita Barrows and Joanna Macy (New York: Riverhead, 1996), 33, no. I, 13.

1. Communal Studies Association, *Guide to Historic Communal Sites in the United States,* 1.
2. Frederick W. Skiff, *Adventures in Americana* (Portland, OR: Metropolitan, 1935), 204.
3. William Keil, "The Letters of Dr. William Keil to the Colony in Bethel, Missouri, 1855," *Sou'wester* 28, no. 4 (Winter 1993): 17–18.
4. Clark M. Will, *The Story of Old Aurora* (Aurora, OR: self-published, 1972), 3.
5. Eugene Edmund Snyder, *Aurora, Their Last Utopia: Oregon's Christian Commune, 1856–1883* (Portland, OR: Binford and Mort, 1993), 63–64.
6. Audrey Ann Buhl, "Clothing and Household Textiles of Aurora Colony, Oregon, 1857 to 1877" (master's thesis, Oregon State University, June 1971), 52. In collection of ACHS.

7. Deborah M. Olsen and Clark M. Will, "Musical Heritage of the Aurora Colony," *Oregon Historical Quarterly* 79, no. 3 (Fall 1978): 235.
8. George Wolfer, quoted in Snyder, *Aurora, Their Last Utopia,* 73, recorded in George Wolfer's diary, ACHS archives.

Part 3: Relationships

Subtitle. Luke 10:29.

Epigraph. Stitched in Time: Thirty-Fourth Annual Quilt Show (Aurora, OR: Aurora Colony Historical Society, 2006).

1. Christian Sherman and Juliana Sherman letter to Sophie Sherman and Catharina Kocher, July 26, 1868, quoted in *Stitched in Time.*
2. Russell Blankenship, *And There Were Men* (New York: Knopf, 1942), 101.
3. Willamette Valley Herb Society, *Emma Wakefield Memorial Herb Garden* (Aurora, OR: Old Aurora Colony Museum).
4. Emma J. Snyder to "my Dear Friend," February 1, 1916, quoted in *Stitched in Time.*
5. *Kenilworth Cook Book* (Portland, OR: Kenilworth Presbyterian Church, 1915), 16.
6. Eugene Edmund Snyder, *Aurora, Their Last Utopia: Oregon's Christian Commune, 1856–1883* (Portland, OR: Binford and Mort, 1993), 123.
7. Quoted in "The Stauffers," *Stitched in Time.*
8. Martha Zimmerman Giesy letter to "My Dear Aunt Mary," August 31, 1901, quoted in *Stitched in Time.*

Part 4: Work

Epigraph. William Bek, "A German Communistic Society in Missouri," *Missouri Historical Review* 3, no. 2 (January 1909): 125, http://shs.umsystem.edu/editorial/mhr/previousabstracts1.shtml.

1. Alison Saar, *Expanded Visions: Four Women Artists Print the American West* (Denver, CO: Women of the West Museum, 2000), 16.

2. Robert Banks and R. Paul Stevens, *The Complete Book of Everyday Christianity: An A-to-Z Guide to Following Christ in Every Aspect of Life* (Downers Grove, IL: InterVarsity, 1997), 240.

3. Banks and Stevens, *Everyday Christianity,* 241.

4. Annette James, in an interview with the author, October 15, 2006.

5. Patrick J. Harris, *Old Aurora Colony,* newsletter (Aurora, OR: Aurora Colony Historical Society, Spring–Summer 2007), 1.

6. Robert J. Hendricks, *Bethel and Aurora: An Experiment in Communism as Practical Christianity* (New York: Press of the Pioneers, 1933), 214–15.

7. Deborah M. Olsen and Clark M. Will, "Musical Heritage of the Aurora Colony," *Oregon Historical Quarterly* 79, no. 3 (Fall 1978): 257.

8. Calvin R. Stapert, *A New Song for an Old World: Musical Thought in the Early Church* (Grand Rapids, MI: Eerdmans, 2007), 201.

9. Stapert, *A New Song,* 53.

10. Olsen and Will, "Musical Heritage of the Aurora Colony," 235.

11. Henry T. Finck, *My Adventures in the Golden Age of Music* (New York: Funk and Wagnalls, 1926), 36.

12. John B. Horner, "Activities of Philomath College," *Oregon Historical Quarterly* 30, no. 4 (December 1929): 345, quoted in Deborah M. Olsen and Clark M. Will, "Musical Heritage of the Aurora Colony," *Oregon Historical Quarterly* 79, no. 3 (Fall 1978): 250.

13. Frederick Woodward Skiff, *Adventures in Americana* (Portland, OR: Metropolitan, 1935), 219.

14. Matthew Deady, *Pharisee Among Philistines,* ed. Malcolm Clark Jr. (Portland, OR: Oregon Historical Society, 1975).

15. Charles Nordhoff, *The Communistic Societies of the United States* (New York: Hillary House, 1961).

16. Finck, *My Adventures,* 39.

17. Finck, *My Adventures,* 39.

18. Finck, *My Adventures,* 27.

19. Finck, *My Adventures,* 39.

Part 5: Faith

1. David Nelson Duke, "A Profile of Religion in the Bethel-Aurora Colonies," *Oregon Historical Quarterly* 92, no. 4 (Winter 1991–92): 348.

2. Duke, "Profile of Religion," 348.

3. Duke, "Profile of Religion," 352–55.

4. Robert J. Hendricks, *Bethel and Aurora: An Experiment in Communism as Practical Christianity* (New York: Press of the Pioneers, 1933), 16–17.

5. Hendricks, *Bethel and Aurora,* 17.

6. Adolf E. Schroeder, *Bethel German Colony, 1844–1883* (St. Louis, MO: Missouri Humanities Council, 1989), quoted in Duke, "Profile of Religion," 354.

7. Hendricks, *Bethel and Aurora,* 207–8.

8. William Bek, "A German Communistic Society in Missouri," *Missouri Historical Review* 3, no. 2 (January 1909): 125.

9. Exhibit placard in the Old Aurora Colony Museum and Robert J. Hendricks, *Bethel and Aurora: An Experiment in Communism as Practical Christianity* (New York: Press of the Pioneers, 1933), 224–26.

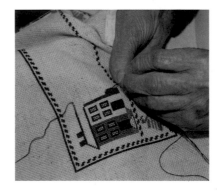

Begin to weave; God provides the thread.

Bibliography

Aurora Colony Historical Society. *Aurora Colony Heritage Recipes.* Aurora, OR: Aurora Colony Historical Society, 1993.

———. *Stitched in Time: Thirty-Fourth Annual Quilt Show.* Aurora, OR: Aurora Colony Historical Society, 2006.

Banks, Robert, and R. Paul Stevens. *The Complete Book of Everyday Christianity: An A-to-Z Guide to Following Christ in Every Aspect of Life.* Downers Grove, IL: InterVarsity, 1997.

Bek, William. "A German Communistic Society in Missouri." *Missouri Historical Review* 3, no. 2 (January 1909): 99–125.

Blankenship, Russell. *And There Were Men.* New York: Knopf, 1942.

Buhl, Audrey Ann. "Clothing and Household Textiles of Aurora Colony, Oregon, 1857 to 1877." Master's thesis, Oregon State University, June 1971. In collection of Aurora Colony Historical Society.

Deady, Matthew. *Pharisees Among Philistines.* Edited by Malcolm Clark Jr. Portland, OR: Oregon Historical Society, 1975.

Downs, Diane Kocher. Telephone interview with the author. November 12, 2007.

Duke, David Nelson. "A Profile of Religion in the Bethel-Aurora Colonies." *Oregon Historical Quarterly* 92, no. 4 (Winter 1991–92): 347–60.

Finck, Henry T. *My Adventures in the Golden Age of Music.* New York: Funk and Wagnalls, 1926.

Hall, Marie Kocher. Interview with the author. Aurora, OR: August 7, 2007.

Harris, Patrick J. Interviews with the author. Aurora, OR: April 2005–September 2008.

Hendricks, Robert J. *Bethel and Aurora: An Experiment in Communism as Practical Christianity.* New York: Press of the Pioneers, 1933.

Horner, John B. "Activities of Philomath College." *Oregon Historical Quarterly* 30, no. 4 (December 1929): 345.

Ihle, Gary and Elaine. Interview with the author. Aurora, OR: July 31, 2007.

James, Annette. Interview with the author. Aurora, OR: October 15, 2006.

Lauria, Jo, and Steve Fenton. *Craft in America.* New York: Clarkson Potter, 2007.

Keil, William. "The Letters of Dr. William Keil to the Colony in Bethel, Missouri, 1855." *Sou'wester* 28, no. 4 (Winter 1993): 3–20.

Kenilworth Presbyterian Church. *Kenilworth Cook Book.* Portland, OR: Kenilworth Presbyterian Church, 1915.

Nordhoff, Charles. *The Communistic Societies of the United States.* New York: Hillary House, 1961.

Old Aurora Colony Museum. *Emma Wakefield Memorial Garden.* Aurora, OR: Old Aurora Colony Museum.

Olsen, Deborah M., and Clark M. Will. "Musical Heritage of the Aurora Colony." *Oregon Historical Quarterly* 79, no. 3 (Fall 1978): 233–37.

Pollard, Lancaster. *Sunday Oregonian.* Portland, OR: October 7, 1956.

Rilke, Rainer Maria. *Rilke's Book of Hours: Love Poems to God.* Translated by Anita Barrows and Joanna Macy. New York: Riverhead, 1996.

Saar, Alison. *Expanded Visions: Four Women Artists Print the American West.* Denver, CO: Women of the West Museum, 2000.

Schriever, Dorothy. Interview with the author. Aurora, OR: August 7, 2007.

Skiff, Frederick W. *Adventures in Americana.* Portland, OR: Metropolitan, 1935.

Snyder, Eugene Edmund. *Aurora, Their Last Utopia: Oregon's Christian Commune, 1856–1883.* Portland, OR: Binford and Mort, 1993.

Stapert, Calvin R. *A New Song for an Old World: Musical Thought in the Early Church.* Grand Rapids, MI: Eerdmans, 2007.

Truman, Michael J. Interview with the author. Portland, OR: November 1, 2007.

Wagner, David. Interviews with the author. Portland, OR: 2005–2008.

Wolfer, George. Diaries. Translated by Clark M. Will. *Sou'wester* 9, no. 3 (Autumn 1974): 43.

Yoder, Vera. Interview with the author. Aurora, OR: August 8, 2007.

Index

Jane Kirkpatrick, an international keynote speaker on the power of stories in our lives, historical women, and the West, blends her clinical social work with her Oregon ranching life and love of history to create award-winning work.

She's the author of three nonfiction books (including this one) and fourteen novels, including the Change and Cherish Historical Series (*A Clearing in the Wild,* a WILLA Literary Award Finalist for Best Historical Novel, 2007; *A Tendering in the Storm,* a Christy finalist for Historical Fiction and winner of the WILLA Literary Award 2008 for Best Original Paperback; and *A Mending at the Edge,* based on some of the stories and people of Aurora), as well as *All Together in One Place, A Name of Her Own* (a BookSense 76 Bookseller's pick), and *A Sweetness to the Soul* (named to Oregon's Literary 100 list of the best one hundred books about Oregon). Her works earn regional and national literary merit, including the prestigious

Wrangler Award from the National Cowboy and Western Heritage Museum, finalist standing for the Oregon Book Award, and Western Writers of America's Best Novel of the West.

Her fifteenth novel, *A Flickering Light,* based on her own grandmother's story, will be released in 2009, the first book in her Portrait of a Woman Series.

Jane lives on Starvation Lane with her husband, Jerry, plus a dog, a cat, and one goat. She can be reached online at www.jkbooks.com and by postal service at 99997 Starvation Lane, Moro, Oregon, 97039.

Author Jane Kirkpatrick with the famous colony Cookie Cutter quilt at the end of a long research day (one of many from 2005 to 2008) at the Frederick Keil colony home in Aurora. *JK photo*